Prostate

Questions You Have... Answers You Need

People's Medical Society Books
Currently Available from Wings Books

Prostate

*Questions
You Have...
Answers
You Need*

by Sandra Salmans

WINGS BOOKS
New York • Avenel, New Jersey

The People's Medical Society is a nonprofit consumer health organization dedicated to the principles of better, more responsive and less expensive medical care. Organized in 1983, the People's Medical Society puts previously unavailable medical information into the hands of consumers so that they can make informed decisions about their own health care.

Membership in the People's Medical Society is $20 a year and includes a subscription to the People's Medical Society Newsletter. For information, write to the People's Medical Society, 462 Walnut Street, Allentown, PA 18102, or call 610-770-1670.

This and other People's Medical Society publications are available for quantity purchase at a discount. Contact the People's Medical Society for details.

This 1994 edition is published by Wings Books, distributed by Random House Value Publishing, Inc., 40 Engelhard Avenue, Avenel, New Jersey 07001, by arrangement with the People's Medical Society.

Random House
New York • Toronto • London • Sydney • Auckland

Printed and bound in the United States of America

Library of Congress Cataloging-in-Publication Data
Salmans, Sandra.
     Prostate: questions you have, answers you need / by Sandra Salmans.
          p.   cm.
     Originally published: Allentown, Pa. : People's Medical Society, 1993.
     Includes bibliographical references and index.
     ISBN 0-517-11931-5
     1. Prostate—Miscellanea. I. Title.
RC899.S256   1994
616.6'5—dc20   94-20914
                                                                CIP

8 7 6 5 4 3 2 1

CONTENTS

INTRODUCTION

Many books are developed out of personal need. Not the need to write, but the need to get information. This book is a perfect illustration.

In January 1993, I went to our family physician because of a minor rash I had developed. He recognized it immediately, prescribed several creams, and suggested that if the problem persisted to call him in a few weeks.

As he looked over my record, he noticed that I had not had a routine physical from him in five years. I indicated that I'd had several for insurance purposes with other practitioners. He suggested that it might not be a bad idea to run a routine blood workup and particularly to run the relatively new PSA (prostate-specific antigen) test, the screening test for prostate cancer. I agreed, since I'd never had that test and did have a case of prostate cancer in my family. His nurse took the blood samples while I was there.

Three days later he sent me a note indicating that my blood work looked great. He noted that my cholesterol level was at 170, well below the "currently acceptable" level of 200. He indicated that it would be another day before the PSA results were back.

Of course, I was happy to get such a good report. But I commented to my wife that night that my low cholesterol report was way below what I usually showed. In fact, it was about 50 points lower than usual. I suggested to her that the test results might have been in error.

The next day I received a second note from my doctor. He again reported how good the report was, but indicated that my PSA results were elevated and should be checked by a urologist. He suggested that I call him to discuss it.

The next morning I called his office and asked about the results. He said the PSA numbers were above normal, indicating that there might be a problem. He suggested I see a urologist as soon as possible. He said he had already spoken to one and that after an examination he might want to take a biopsy of the prostate gland. I told him that I would make an appointment right away and that I wanted him to send me written copies of all the test results.

But I also informed him of my suspicion of an error with this test. I noted that my cholesterol level was well below its usual level. He didn't think so.

Three days later I went to visit the urologist. Before examining me, he asked about my family history and if I had any symptoms that might reveal a prostate problem (I had none). He then explained that a normal level on the PSA test is a range of 1 to 4. My result was between 11 and 12. Such a high level, he said, is a strong indication that prostate cancer might be present. He then proceeded to tell me that he believed in aggressively treating the problem. He talked about the digital exam he would now give me. Next would be a biopsy performed at the hospital. Then he talked about his recommended approach to the treatment of prostate cancer.

I sat through his lecture with growing trepidation. I could feel the color draining from my face as beads of sweat formed on my forehead. The words passing through my mind were "cancer," "death" and "family." I even started to feel faint.

But the longer he talked the more rational I became. First, I realized that he had not even examined me. Second, I kept thinking that the test might be in error. Third, I had not done any research on the matter myself.

When he finished talking I told him that I would let him perform a digital examination right now. However,

I told him that if he felt nothing unusual I wanted to have another blood test taken at a different laboratory. I told him why I suspected a testing error. He agreed, but told me that he had never seen that happen.

He performed the digital examination and found nothing unusual. I told him I wanted the second blood test.

Five days later I had the blood test. Two days later the results came back. My PSA count was 1.4. The urologist was amazed. He said he had never seen such a mistake happen before.

I called our family practitioner, who also was shocked. I suggested that he check the records of his patients that day who had blood sent to the laboratory. I also noted to him that there had been a gentleman in his late 80s sitting in his reception room waiting to be picked up. I thought our blood samples may have been mixed up.

After several weeks of checking it was discovered that the error had been made at the laboratory used by my family physician. All of the blood samples from his office had been mixed up at the lab. The lab, by the way, is one of the nation's largest. And it appears that I was right— I got the older man's results.

As you can readily imagine, my own anxiety and the worry felt by my family for the two weeks that this took to get resolved was significant. I may not have been right; I very well could have had prostate cancer. But I was right. My own suspicions were borne out.

During this ordeal, I scoured library and bookstore shelves for as much information as I could find about prostate-related problems, tests used in diagnosis, and treatment options. I found a little bit of information here and a little more there. What was lacking was one easy-to-understand yet comprehensive book that answered my questions. I decided that the People's Medical Society would publish such a book. This is it.

Prostate: Questions You Have . . . Answers You Need is another in a series of similar books we began producing several years ago. The response to these books has been tremendous. Consumers write or call to let us know just how useful and informative each book is. They applaud

the question-and-answer format. But even more important, they appreciate the depth we go into dealing with
each subject.

Health writer Sandra Salmans, who authored this book
for the People's Medical Society, has done extensive research on every aspect of prostate-related issues. And she
has translated her findings into language that any person
wanting such information will find easy to understand.
I know. I put it to the test.

The story I related above underscores the importance
of being alert and involved in your own medical care. My
family practitioner and the urologist were convinced the
test could not be mistaken. Even though I presented no
symptoms, they did not want to dispute the test results.
Neither had ever experienced a laboratory making such a
big mistake. Frankly, I am sure it has happened to them
before, but they never realized it and mistakenly treated
people for conditions they never had.

Even if my test results had been the right ones, I was
still lacking in information. I had to look deep into the
medical literature to find out the accuracy of the PSA test.
I had to search many technical articles to find out the
latest thinking on the treatment of prostate cancer. No
consumer should have to do that. The information should
be easily available and understandable.

Since 1983, the People's Medical Society has been filling
a critical need: to provide the important information consumers must have to work in partnership with their own
practitioners. Without such, making wise and informed
medical decisions is impossible.

Charles B. Inlander
President
People's Medical Society

Prostate

*Questions
You Have...
Answers
You Need*

Terms printed in boldface can be found in the glossary, beginning on page 169. Only the first mention of the word in the text will be boldfaced.

We have tried to use male and female pronouns in an egalitarian manner throughout the book. Any imbalance in usage has been in the interest of readability.

1 A PRIMER ON THE PROSTATE

Q: First things first. What is the **prostate?**

A: Probably not what you think it is. Most people, if they've heard of the prostate at all, think it's a male sex organ. It's not, although it's in the vicinity. The prostate is actually a **gland** of the male reproductive system, located in front of the **rectum** and at the base of the **bladder** (the organ that stores urine). The prostate surrounds a part of the **urethra**, the tube that carries urine from the bladder out through the penis.

Sometimes people who have a vague idea what the prostate is—who know, anyway, that it's not a sex organ—confuse it with the **prostatic urethra**. That's the portion of the urethra that's within the prostate. And while we're on the subject of anatomy, here's a little more: The prostatic urethra ends at the external **urethral sphincter**, the muscle you voluntarily contract when you're urinating and want to stop the flow suddenly. There's another sphincter at the opening of the bladder, which operates involuntarily. Both function as valve mechanisms that provide urinary control in men.

Q: What does a prostate look like?

A: In an adult male, the prostate is about the size and shape of a large walnut and weighs about 20 grams, or a little less than one ounce. If you looked at it under a microscope, you'd see a mass of muscle, glands and connective tissue. The outer surface of the prostate is covered by thick muscle, often called the prostatic capsule because it encapsulates, or encases, the gland.

While there isn't any actual demarcation within the prostate itself, doctors often speak of the gland as being made up of "lobes" or "zones." The central zone surrounds the urethra. A larger, peripheral zone envelops the central zone. And a small but medically important transitional zone lies within the central zone, adjacent to the urethral sphincter. When they examine the prostate for disease, doctors refer to these lobes or zones.

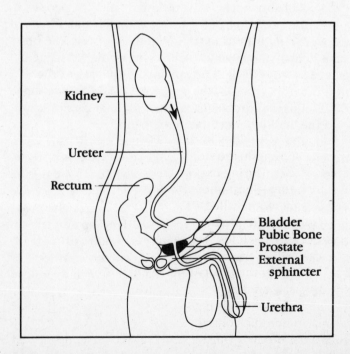

Q: So if the prostate's not a sex organ, what does it do?

A: As we said, it's a gland, because the definition of gland is something that produces secretions. But it's a pretty sexy gland, and its main role in life is sexual reproduction.

Around the same time that a boy's **testicles** develop the ability to produce sperm, the prostate gland becomes mature enough to produce the seminal fluid that will support the sperm. There are lots of small glands within the prostate, and they're producing and storing secretions more or less continuously. In fact, the prostate makes about 90 percent of the milky semen in which spermatozoa travel outside the body during orgasm and ejaculation.

Q: So the sperm travel through the prostate?

A: It's a bit more complicated than that. At the risk of giving you another lesson in the birds and the bees, here's precisely what happens. We go into more detail than you need right now, because some of the anatomical parts we name here are going to play roles later in this book.

As every schoolboy knows, the testes manufacture sperm. The sperm are stored in a structure called the **epididymis**. During orgasm, another structure, called the **vas deferens**—best-known as the subjects of the contraceptive operation called **vasectomy**—push the sperm into the prostatic urethra. The sperm swim in fluid from the **seminal vesicles**, which are two saclike structures directly behind the base of the bladder. At the same time, the muscles of the prostate contract, pouring fluid into the prostatic urethra.

This broth of fluids is then propelled out, or ejaculated, by the spasmodic contractions of the muscles that surround the urethra. During sexual intercourse, the semen carries the sperm into the woman's vagina and uterus, and up into the fallopian tubes in order to fertilize an egg.

Q: Does the prostatic fluid serve any other purpose?

A: It supplies some nourishment to the fragile sperm. It's also thought that the fluid helps make the vaginal canal less acidic. All that increases the likelihood of conception.

Q: So . . . no prostate, no sex, no baby?

A: It's a common misconception, if you'll excuse the pun, that men who develop prostatic problems can't have erections. The specter of impotence seems to loom over every uninformed discussion of prostate.

The good news is that the vast majority of men who are treated for prostatic disease are able to perform as well sexually as they did before. The bad news is that there's a minority of men whose sexual performance is permanently impaired. As for conception, obviously if there's no semen, there's no easy way of getting sperm to egg. But there are other ways, and we address all these important issues later in more detail.

Q: Sounds like the prostate can be troublesome. Is that true?

A: In Chapter 2, we discuss all the things that can go wrong with the prostate gland. Suffice it to say, for now, that the prostate causes more misery for men than just about any other structure in the body. And

sexual performance is affected less than other, more hum-
drum functions—notably urination. More than half of all
American men eventually develop enlarged prostates,
some of which ultimately require surgery or other treatment. Approximately one in nine American men develops
prostate cancer during his lifetime, and some 35,000
die of it each year. All that trouble from a seemingly
innocuous little gland!

Q: **How can I tell if something's wrong with
my prostate?**

A: The most common symptom is a urinary problem.
You may find that you need to urinate more often,
especially at night. You may have trouble starting the
urine flow. Once it's started, you may have trouble
stopping it. Urine may trickle out, stop and start again.
Depending on the particular disease, you may have pain
or burning when you urinate, chills and fever, and pain in
the lower back, pelvis or upper thighs. You may also have
watery or brownish discharges from your penis that are
different from the secretions your prostate normally
produces. Sometimes you'll have **hematuria**, or blood
in the urine.

Q: **So if I have a prostate problem, I'll have one
or more of these symptoms?**

A: Not necessarily. It's possible to develop a prostatic
disease and have no symptoms for a while. That's
particularly true with cancer of the prostate, which grows
slowly and in its early stages typically doesn't produce
any symptoms that signal its presence. Often cancer is
detected during a routine **digital (manual) rectal exam**
or surgery for an altogether different prostatic condition.

Q: What's a rectal exam?

A: It's a simple, relatively painless exam that takes about a minute and can be done by either your family doctor or a **urologist**, a specialist in diseases of the urinary tract and the male reproductive system. While you bend at the waist and lean over an examining table or chair, the doctor inserts a lubricated, gloved finger up your rectum to the point where he can feel your prostate.

The exam is such a standard and important part of men's health care that it's sometimes known as the "male Pap smear," after the widely used screening test for cervical cancer in women.

Q: What does it show?

A: The exam may reveal a great deal. A normal prostate feels smooth and elastic. The presence of lumps or other areas of abnormal texture, or a prostate that's rock-hard, may well point to cancer. If the prostate is enlarged, it could indicate the onset of **benign prostatic hyperplasia (BPH)**. That's a prostatic condition that afflicts most men as they age. In it, the prostate grows, choking the prostatic urethra and obstructing the flow of urine. We discuss BPH in detail in the next chapter.

Q: How often should I have a rectal exam?

A: There's some disagreement over the age at which a man should have his first rectal exam, and how frequently such exams should take place after that. The American Cancer Society (ACS) recommends a rectal exam each year for all men over the age of 40—or in their late 30s if they're in any high-risk group.

Many doctors start the clock ticking about 10 years later. They advise a rectal exam every year for men over 50 or, if there's prostate cancer in the family, yearly exams starting at 40. Some health authorities, not including the ACS, think that men who are 70 or more and have no symptoms can give up routine rectal exams, because the prostatic cancer the doctor would be looking for tends to progress so slowly that the men are likely to die first of other causes.

According to the ACS, less than half of all American men who should have routine examinations do so. Even using many physicians' more relaxed guidelines, that means there are a lot of men who aren't taking care of themselves.

Q: Are there other physical exams?

A: Depending on what he's looking for, the doctor may press on your bladder or examine your penis and testicles. But the rectal exam is the primary physical exam. In addition, there's a battery of diagnostic tests you can take, depending on your symptoms.

Q: The one urological test I've heard about is something called **cystoscopy**. What is it?

A: It's a procedure that involves passing a cystoscope —a slender, hollow tube with a light and a lens on one end, and a viewing lens on the other—through the opening in the penis, into the urethra and then into the bladder.

Cystoscopy is an exceptionally valuable procedure because it helps doctors diagnose most of the diseases that ail the prostate. By looking through various lenses, doctors can see the interior of the prostatic urethra and diagnose inflammation. If a prostate is enlarged, cystoscopy can indicate the degree of obstruction in the prostatic urethra, the size and weight of the obstructing prostatic tissue, and any **urinary retention** (or how much urine is retained in the bladder because it can't get through the urethra). The cystoscope is also used in patients with prostatic cancer, to locate sources of prostatic bleeding and to assess how much the tumor is impinging on the urethra.

Q: Isn't that terribly painful—having a tube up my penis?

A: A cystoscopy sounds pretty awful, but most men who've undergone the exam say the anticipation is worse than the reality. The newest cystoscopes are more flexible than the original models, making them less uncomfortable. In any event, the procedure can be done with a local anesthetic and, if you're especially nervous, a sedative, too.

However, you should be aware that cystoscopy, like any procedure of this type, carries the risk of infection. In many cases, there are other tests that serve the purpose just as well. Some urologists perform cystoscopy only under special circumstances, such as to evaluate blood in a patient's urine.

Q: What are some of those other tests?

A: Since we've been talking so much about urine, you won't be surprised to hear that **urinalysis** tops the list. An analysis of your urine can show whether any bacteria or white cells are present, indicating infection.

The urine test may be a somewhat elaborate, three-cup affair that allows the doctor to analyze the first urine you void, your "midstream" urine, and a third sample that contains prostatic fluid.

If you report trouble urinating, the doctor may use a machine to measure your urine flow rate. She may also **catheterize** your bladder—insert a long rubber tube up the urethra—to measure urinary retention.

Q: What about blood tests and x-rays?

A: There are any number of blood tests that evaluate how well the kidneys are functioning and that look for prostate cancer. One that you'll read a lot about in this book is called the **prostate-specific antigen (PSA)** test.

Imaging and **biopsy** are two other diagnostic tools that may be used. They can help to determine the presence or extent of prostate cancer or can provide information about the urinary tract prior to surgery. But we're getting ahead of ourselves. Let's talk about the different diseases that come under the heading "prostate trouble" and the specific tests that help diagnose them.

2 PROSTATIC DISEASE

Q: What is prostatic disease?

A: In reality, three different types of disease affect the prostate gland. Two are benign conditions—that is, they're not usually life-threatening. And it's easy to confuse them, at least initially, because they produce many of the same symptoms.

Prostatitis is an inflammation of the prostate, often caused by a bacterial infection. While it is true that bacteria cause some types of prostatitis, no microbe has been held accountable for other types. Whatever its cause, prostatitis can occur in men of any age and generally responds to medication or other treatment.

Benign prostatic hyperplasia (BPH), which we mentioned briefly in Chapter 1, is a noncancerous enlargement of the prostate. It's the most common form of prostatic disease: More than half of men over 50 have enlarged prostates.

Prostate cancer, which you also read a little about earlier, is a potentially serious disease because it's a malignant condition. That means that, over time, the cancer cells multiply without control, forming too much tissue and invading and destroying healthy cells nearby.

While prostate cancer can occur in men of all ages, 80 percent occurs in men who are 65 or more. Approximately
one in nine American men develops prostate cancer, and
some 35,000 die each year from this disease.

In this chapter, we explore each of these diseases in
detail. However, the treatment options only for prostatitis
are addressed here. In Chapters 3 and 4, we discuss treatments for BPH and prostate cancer.

PROSTATITIS

Q: Okay, run that by me again—what is
prostatitis?

A: Strictly speaking, it's inflammation of the prostate.
Bacteria or some other microorganism can cause
the disease, or it can result from factors other than bacteria.

So there are two kinds of prostatitis: nonbacterial, or
noninfectious; and bacterial, or infectious. We'll cut out
some of the medical verbiage and refer to the two categories from here on as **nonbacterial prostatitis** and
bacterial prostatitis. But first we should note that
"prostatitis" is often used as a catchall term for a handful
of different urinary-tract infections and conditions.
Because of the way the urethra, bladder and prostate are
connected, conditions affecting one or another often
have similar or overlapping symptoms.

Q: What's nonbacterial prostatitis?

A: It's the most common kind of prostatitis and, as
its name suggests, isn't a disease or an infection
but a condition. Doctors generally divide nonbacterial

prostatitis into two categories: **Congestive prostatitis** (sometimes called **prostatostasis**—literally, ''condition of the prostate'') is the most common; the other is **prostatodynia** (which means ''painful prostate'').

Congestive prostatitis occurs when too much prostatic fluid, the milky fluid that goes into semen, accumulates within the prostate gland rather than being ejaculated out of the body. It's said that the prostate is ''congested'' or ''engorged.''

Prostatodynia is the term used to describe a condition in which pain seems to be originating in the prostate, but is much more likely to be coming from the muscles of the floor of the pelvis, from an inflammation in one or more of the pelvic bones, or from a disease in the rectum. In this condition, the prostate itself is probably normal.

Q: Why does the prostate become congested?

A: Some practitioners believe that chronic, unrelenting stress is responsible for most cases of prostatic disease, particularly when there's no sign of a bacteria or virus. And some scientists are still searching for a mystery microorganism.

But in the absence of other evidence, other eminent urologists have concluded that sex—too much or too little—is to blame. That's the hunch of Stephen N. Rous, M.D., author of *The Prostate Book,* and the late Monroe E. Greenberger, M.D., author of *What Every Man Should Know About His Prostate.*

Remember that old husbands' tale (we'll call it that because we're sure it wasn't an old wives' tale!) that a man could become ill if he didn't have enough sex? Some caddish fellows used it to persuade reluctant virgins to go to bed with them. Well, in these experts' view, there may be some truth to the story.

Every day a healthy prostate secretes between one-tenth and two-fifth teaspoon of prostatic fluid. When you're sexually aroused, however, you produce between 4 and 10 times that amount. Normally, you release it through ejaculation. But if you don't ejaculate, the fluid builds up and the prostate becomes congested.

Q: But what about men who never ejaculate? Do they get congestive prostatitis?

A: Nonbacterial prostatitis has been called the disease of popes and priests, but it's probably caused more by an abrupt change in sexual habits than by celibacy. Suppose you're used to ejaculating on a fairly regular basis of, say, three times weekly. Then, for whatever reason—maybe you had a falling out with your sexual partner or one of you is ill or traveling—the rate drops to once a week or less. Your prostate gland has become "programmed" to secrete merrily at the three-times-a-week rate, but now the fluid has nowhere to go. So the gland swells up.

Q: Are there other causes of congestive prostatitis?

A: Greenberger has suggested that the condition can also be caused by **coitus interruptus**, which may diminish the volume of ejaculation, and by chronic vibration, which seems to give the prostate the illusion that intercourse is imminent and leads it to secrete fluid. Bus drivers and motorcycle police are among the people whose jobs predispose them to congestive prostatitis.

Q: Okay. But how can too much sex be bad for my prostate?

A: Suppose you've been celibate for a long period, then have an extremely active weekend. Your prostate, which has become used to a low rate of secretion, is suddenly required to produce fluid for several ejaculations. This isn't a case of a congested prostate, just an extremely irritated one.

Q: What causes prostatodynia?

A: It's not clear, although some physicians think it's stress related. Sometimes examinations show that the bladder neck and urethral sphincter—one of the muscles that controls urination—are hypertonic, or tense. Ira Sharlip, M.D., a urologist and assistant clinical professor at the University of California Medical Center in San Francisco, has said that, in the absence of bacteria, "most prostatitis is actually urinary sphincter hypertonicity."

Q: What's bacterial prostatitis?

A: Again, the name gives it away: a prostatic disease caused by a bacterial infection in the prostate. And, like the nonbacterial variety, bacterial prostatitis takes two forms: acute and chronic. Both are pretty uncommon.

Acute bacterial prostatitis is a rare and serious illness, not to be confused with the garden-variety prostatic conditions we've just described. It results from a sudden infusion of bacteria into the prostate gland, either by direct extension from an infection in the urethra or, very occasionally, by a bloodborne spread of bacteria from an infection elsewhere in the body.

Chronic bacterial prostatitis is, as the name suggests, a recurring infection in the prostate. It's probably the result of residual infection when acute bacterial prostatitis hasn't been knocked out of the system.

Q: What are the bacteria that cause these infections?

A: The most common prostatic infection—and remember, bacterial prostatitis is fairly uncommon —comes from **colon bacilli**, or bacteria that are in the colon. They get into the prostate directly from the rectum or through the bloodstream.

Q: How do you pick up the bug?

A: Not from a toilet seat, but that's about the only category you can exclude. You can get the bacteria by swimming in unclean pools or beaches or by drinking dirty water. It's also possible, although unlikely, to pick it up from a bacterial infection elsewhere in the body, like a sinus infection, tonsillitis, an abscessed tooth or an ear infection.

Q: How else?

A: You can also develop bacterial prostatitis if you already have an enlarged prostate, or the condition known as BPH that's so common in older men. When the prostate reaches a certain size, the obstruction may make it impossible for you to empty your bladder completely. Bacteria can grow in the stagnant urine that remains. That may lead to a bladder infection, which occasionally spreads to the prostate.

By the same token, you're at a higher risk for getting bacterial prostatitis if you've recently had a urinary catheter inserted to drain urine from your bladder.

Q: Can bacterial prostatitis be sexually transmitted?

A: No. Although bacterial prostatitis is an infection, it's not contagious. So you can't give it to your sexual partner.

However, a number of infections transmitted during sexual intercourse, including **gonorrhea** and candida— the latter is a common infection that you probably know as a yeast infection—can lead to bacterial prostatitis. Anal intercourse may be the worst culprit, because it can send bacteria-laden feces into the bloodstream.

Q: It sounds like it's pretty easy to get infected. True?

A: Not really. The prostate is in a capsule that's not easily penetrated, so it's fairly well protected against infections. But when microorganisms do get in, they find the prostate's a good host. The **blood-prostate barrier**, which keeps certain substances from penetrating the prostate, also keeps out most antibiotics. So once the prostate is infected, it can be extremely difficult to clear. Then the prostate becomes more and more inflamed, and it gets even harder to eradicate bacteria.

Q: What other forms of prostatitis are there?

A: Strictly speaking, we've just run through the list. However, as we said earlier, the term is often applied to other conditions with similar symptoms. The main one is **nonspecific urethritis (NSU)**, a fairly common infection of the prostatic urethra. It's usually caused by **chlamydia**, the most common sexually transmitted disease. However, there are other bugs that can work the same mischief.

Urethritis, if left untreated, may progress to a kidney infection, but it's generally caught long before then. For our purposes here, the most important thing about urethritis is that it can lead to acute bacterial prostatitis.

Q: What are the symptoms of prostatitis?

A: Although there are some variations, both non-bacterial and bacterial prostatitis share many of the same symptoms. With both conditions, you might expect to find that your penis seems to be "glued" shut when you wake up in the morning. When you open it, you'll probably notice a drop or two of clear liquid. At the end of the day, you may find a brownish or yellowish stain, about the size of a dime or a quarter, in your underpants.

You may also get a feeling of discomfort or itching deep inside your penis. And you may feel some discomfort when you urinate. If you've had much to do with the medical profession, you've probably concluded that discomfort is a popular euphemism for pain. But if you've ever urinated with a kidney stone, you know the difference.

Q: All that itching and dripping sounds like venereal disease. How can I tell the difference?

A: It is confusing, particularly since, as we said earlier, gonorrhea can lead to prostatitis. But the early signs are different. Gonorrhea affects what's called the anterior portion of the urethra, the part that's within the penis rather than the part that's enclosed by the prostate. So if you have gonorrhea, the itching and discomfort will be toward the end of your penis.

Q: Are there any other symptoms?

A: Yes, depending on the condition. If it's nonbacterial prostatitis, the prostate may be swollen or engorged. Temporarily, that creates the same problem you encounter with benign prostatic hyperplasia: It becomes difficult to urinate.

With prostatodynia, there's usually pain or discomfort in the **perineum** (the area between the **scrotum** and the **anus**), in the rectum or in the area just above the pubic hair line.

Q: Are the symptoms always mild?

A: Not if you've got acute bacterial prostatitis. In that case, you can run a fever of 102° or higher. You may have the malaise, aches and pains usually associated with flu. And often you'll develop low abdominal or lower-back pain. The infection makes the prostate gland swell, too, so it may be difficult or even impossible to urinate.

Q: Is prostatitis serious?

A: Not usually, except for acute bacterial prostatitis. Having prostatitis doesn't increase your risk of getting any other prostatic disease, including cancer. Nor, contrary to many men's instinctive reaction, does it lead to impotence.

Q: Do you mean it's not necessary to see a doctor?

A: No, merely that it's not an emergency. Because the symptoms of the various forms of prostatitis, except for acute bacterial prostatitis, are so similar, it's important to take tests that pinpoint a diagnosis. Before you start a course of antibiotics, first you need to make sure you've even got a bacterial infection. Chances are, you don't. Besides, if you start antibiotics before you have a complete **urine culture**, it can become difficult to make a proper diagnosis.

Q: What tests does a doctor perform?

A: In most cases, the first thing a doctor will do is perform a rectal exam. If the prostate feels somewhat enlarged and spongy, it could be nonbacterial prostatitis. And if the sexual history you provide shows a recent erratic—as opposed to erotic!—pattern, that's confirmation.

If you're showing signs of acute bacterial prostatitis, however, the doctor should perform the rectal exam gingerly, or perhaps not at all. For one thing, the prostate would be extremely tender and painful. But more important, too much pressure on the prostate might propel the infection into the testicles, epididymis or bloodstream, causing severe systemic infection.

Q: Besides the rectal exam, what would he do?

A: He'll almost certainly do a urinalysis to check your urine for signs of infection, such as white cells and bacteria. If your urine is teeming with bacteria, you probably have acute bacterial prostatitis.

To diagnose chronic bacterial prostatitis, he'll need a slightly more elaborate test—actually a series of tests called a **segmented urine culture**. First you'll urinate into a cup. Then you'll do a midstream urination. Next the doctor will insert his gloved finger into your rectum and massage or "strip" the prostate to release prostatic secretions. This isn't a painful procedure, but it is fairly uncomfortable. Finally, you'll urinate into a third cup. Because of the prostatic massage, the third urine sample will contain prostatic fluid.

The doctor will culture all three urine samples. If the urine sample containing prostatic fluid has a high bacteria count, a diagnosis of chronic bacterial prostatitis is reasonable. On the other hand, if the bacteria counts for the first and third urine samples are equally high, it's probably urethritis rather than prostatitis.

Q: What about a cystoscopy?

A: A cystoscopy could show inflammation of the prostatic urethra, which would confirm a diagnosis of urethritis or possible bacterial prostatitis. But in the vast majority of cases, a careful urinalysis should suffice.

Q: So I take antibiotics, right?

A: It depends on what you've got. Unfortunately, there's almost a kneejerk reaction that, when prostatitis is diagnosed, you take antibiotics. But most people won't respond because there's actually no infection and no bacteria. Then they run the risk of being on antibiotics for months, pouring money down a hole and possibly developing side effects, and yet still have the problem.

Q: But there are cases where antibiotics work?

A: Sure. For acute bacterial prostatitis, you typically take antibiotics for several weeks. Depending on how severe the symptoms are, you may also be put on **analgesics** to relieve pain and be ordered to bed. You may even be hospitalized and put on intravenous antibiotics because of the danger that the infection may spread to the bloodstream. Or you may be hospitalized if your prostate is so swollen that you're completely unable to urinate, or if you need intravenous fluids because you're running a high fever.

And there'll be careful follow-up. The problem with this infection is that it's virtually impossible to be sure it's cured. So you may find it coming back, time and again, as chronic bacterial prostatitis, and each time it's more difficult to cure.

Q: What happens then? More antibiotics?

A: If you have chronic bacterial prostatitis, you usually are treated with a combination of sulfa and trimethoprim (you may recognize the brand names, like Bactrim and Septra), or with other drugs, depending upon the bacteria's sensitivity to antibiotics. If the infection is particularly stubborn, you may stay on antibiotics for three months or more. There are cases where men have been on continuous antibiotic therapy for years.

Q: What if antibiotics don't get rid of chronic bacterial prostatitis?

A: For particularly resistant cases of chronic bacterial prostatitis, researchers are investigating the injection of antibiotics directly into the prostate. A group of Belgian doctors have reported that up to 60 percent of men who had received such injections responded well for at least six months. While the treatment can be somewhat uncomfortable, the benefits probably outweigh the discomfort or risk of long-term antibiotic therapy. However, the therapy is still very experimental at this point.

In extreme cases, your doctor may advise either a partial or a complete **prostatectomy**, or surgical removal of the prostate. Clearly it's the last resort. Surgery might be called for if you're developing urinary retention or kidney problems as a result of prostatitis. Or maybe, because you've had frequent prostate infections, you've acquired a tendency to develop stones in the gland. The stones become contaminated, and that perpetuates the prostatitis. We have more to say about surgical options in Chapter 3.

Q: How is nonbacterial prostatitis treated?

A: If it's congestive prostatitis, both Greenberger and Rous say you should treat yourself to a romp in bed. After all, if the condition is the result of a buildup of fluid, the remedy is to release the fluid, or to ejaculate.

If that's not an option, these urologists add, well, take matters into your own hands, so to speak. Some men who are reluctant to masturbate may feel less guilt-ridden if they know it's doctor's orders.

If neither sex nor masturbation is possible, another option is prostate massage, which we described as part of the test for prostatitis and which can be done in a doctor's office. Like ejaculation, it has the effect of releasing seminal fluid and relieving congestion.

Q: What about prostatodynia?

A: As we said earlier, it's a condition that's often thought to be stress related, so the remedies are, too. Physicians often prescribe muscle relaxants. In some cases, they may also recommend tranquilizers or psychotherapy. If the pelvic area appears inflamed, they may recommend over-the-counter anti-inflammatory medications like ibuprofen or aspirin.

Q: What if I just ignore the symptoms?

A: With nonbacterial prostatitis, it's possible to grin and bear it. But apart from the fact that there's no point in suffering pain needlessly, there's some evidence that nonbacterial prostatitis can make a man more susceptible to bacterial prostatitis.

Q: What about diet or self-help remedies?

A: There's what doctors call anecdotal evidence—based on patients' reports rather than on clinical studies—that certain beverages, like coffee, gin, whiskey and red wine, and spicy foods, irritate the prostate and can promote a flare-up of prostatitis. (It may not be coincidental that these same drinks and foods also irritate the bladder.) Some men also report that heavy lifting, vigorous exercise and especially prolonged driving can worsen the symptoms.

We've already mentioned some treatments for prostatodynia you can administer yourself. Another popular treatment is a hot sitz bath, which draws more blood to the area, increases local circulation and relaxes the muscles. **Biofeedback** has also helped some people.

Q: I've heard that zinc is good for the prostate. True?

A: Some experts believe that zinc may act as a defense against prostate infection, for both prevention and therapy. Zinc is found in high concentration in seminal fluid and in the prostate itself. In fact, there's more zinc in the prostate than in any other place in the body.

Researchers have found that, in the laboratory, the amount of zinc normally present in prostatic fluid is effective against various types of bacteria. At the same time, they've noted that patients with chronic prostatitis have either little or no zinc in their prostatic secretions. Some experts believe that the drop in zinc concentration precedes any bacterial invasion, rather than bacteria causing a drop in zinc levels.

Q: How much zinc should I take?

A: First of all, there's considerable debate over whether you should take zinc at all. Many researchers believe that the prostate does not pick up zinc from the bloodstream when it's taken in pill form.

Having said that, we'll add that there's another school of thought that zinc supplements are worthwhile. Those urologists recommend zinc sulfate tablets (zinc gluconate, which many people take to fight colds, is not effective) in doses of about 50 milligrams a day. You can also eat zinc-rich foods like oysters, nuts, pumpkin seeds, wheat germ and bran, milk, eggs, chicken, peas, lentils and beef liver. (Of course, some of those foods are also high in fat and cholesterol and are to be avoided for that reason.)

Certain individuals need more zinc than others: people with diabetes, heavy drinkers and, according to some doctors, people undergoing unusual stress. Before you step up your dosage, however, you should consult a physician —or, if alcohol is the issue, cut back your drinking.

And some doctors warn that, while small amounts of zinc may boost the body's immune system, extremely large amounts may make it more difficult for the body to defend itself against infection and may lower your resistance to cancer.

Q: Are there any other self-help remedies?

A: One homeopathic treatment that's favored is cold-pressed linseed oil. Another treatment is a pollen preparation called cernitin. Pollen tablets are available at drug and health-food stores. For more information about such remedies, consult homeopathy guides and your local health-food store.

BENIGN PROSTATIC HYPERPLASIA (BPH)

Q: What is benign prostatic hyperplasia?

A: It's a noncancerous enlargement of the prostate gland. Hyperplasia is a nontumorous increase in the number of cells in an organ or tissue, so that the organ or tissue grows in size. The phrase is a mouthful, so from here on, we refer to the condition as BPH.

Q: You mean the prostate is actually growing?

A: That's right. When a boy is born, his prostate is about the size of a pea. It grows very slowly until puberty, when there's a period of rapid growth that continues for several years, until the prostate reaches its normal adult size. It remains that size until about age 40 or 45. At that point, the prostate begins to grow again, and continues growing until death.

Q: How large does it get?

A: On average, it might peak at about 33 grams, or 1½ ounces. That's fairly small. Still, it's an increase of 50 percent over the prostate's normal size. (The largest reported prostate size in a man with BPH was 1,058 grams, but that's the stuff of medical case studies.)

Q: **Is BPH cancer?**

A: No. As the term says, the condition is benign, not malignant. If you looked at both normal prostate tissue and BPH tissue under a microscope, you'd see that BPH tissue generally has more glands and less muscle and connective tissue. But for all practical purposes, there's no difference between the two kinds of tissue.

Q: **If the growth is benign, what's the big deal?**

A: As they say in real estate, it all comes down to location, location, location. An enlarged prostate can have a stranglehold on the urethra.

Think of the urethra as a straw that runs from the bladder to the end of the penis, draining urine from the body. BPH begins right up against the wall of the prostatic urethra (the part of the urethra that passes through the prostate). If growth is outward, away from the urethra, and even if the prostate becomes as large as a tennis ball, it's not a problem. But if the new growth is inward, the prostate presses in on the urethra, squeezing it and making urination increasingly difficult.

Q: **Is BPH common?**

A: Very, and becoming more so all the time, as life expectancy rises. It's been called the disease of old men—one of the most famous prostate patients in recent years was President Ronald Reagan who, at the age of 76, had surgery for BPH in 1987—but it afflicts plenty of not-so-old men, too.

Q: What are the actual odds of my developing BPH?

A: In the flurry of statistics, it might sound as though anybody who lives long enough to grow a few gray hairs is doomed. So it's useful to distinguish between an obstructive prostate and one that's merely enlarged. Autopsy studies show that over half of all men who are 50 years or more and about three-quarters of men who are 70 or over have BPH. By age 80, the incidence is even higher.

That doesn't mean that the men died from the condition —just that it was present when they died. It also doesn't mean that the enlargement was progressive, or that they had any symptoms. Stephen N. Rous, the urologist we mentioned earlier, estimates in *The Prostate Book* that between one-quarter and one-half "of those men who have anatomic changes of BPH will also have the symptoms which will send them to their physicians." That averages out to about one in six men over the age of 50, and about one in three over the age of 70.

That's a minority, but it's still a big number. It's been said that BPH accounts for urinary problems in about 10 million men in the United States over the age of 50. According to the National Center for Health Statistics, each year the condition is responsible for 1.7 million doctor's-office visits and some 400,000 operations.

Q: Whew! Is there anyone who doesn't get BPH?

A: There seem to be two groups of men who are impervious to the disease, and it's their characteristics that provide us with a lot of information about the causes of BPH and how it might be treated.

The first group consists of men who've been castrated— that is, they've had their testicles removed surgically or

shrunk by taking female hormones such as **estrogen**—
and no longer produce **testosterone**. These men's
immunity to BPH led doctors years ago to the conclusion
that enlargement of the prostate gland is somehow related
to the production of testosterone.

About 100 years ago, in fact, men with obstructive BPH
were sometimes castrated as a way of relieving their symptoms, and doctors boasted that their patients improved
àt rates of 80 to 87 percent. But that might have been a
case where the cure was worse than the disease. Once
surgical remedies were introduced, castration went out.

Q: What about the other group that doesn't
get BPH?

A: Those are men who have normal testosterone
levels but in whom BPH just does not develop.
Not only do these men have small prostates throughout
their lives, but their prostates actually decrease slowly in
volume as they age. Although in other ways the men are
normal, they have less facial and less body hair than the
average male, and they don't grow bald.

It's been found that these men have a genetically linked
deficiency of an enzyme called **5-alpha-reductase**. That
enzyme converts testosterone into a more active **androgen**,
or male hormone, called **dihydrotestosterone (DHT)**.

Q: Does that mean DHT makes the prostate grow?

A: Nobody knows for certain what leads to BPH,
although it seems clear that a combination of aging
and hormones is responsible. But, yes, the main theory
these days centers on the role of DHT.

The concentration of DHT in the normal prostate and
in seminal vesicles is much higher than in other tissues.

And DHT concentrations in BPH tissue that's removed during surgery are higher than those seen in normal prostate tissue. Moreover, in test-tube studies, DHT has been shown to stimulate hyperplasia in prostate cells.

Most animals lose their ability to produce DHT as they age. Men produce less testosterone as they age, but they continue to produce and accumulate high levels of DHT in the prostate.

Q: What do scientists believe actually happens?

A: The belief is that DHT is transported to the nuclei of the prostate cells, where it sets off a cascade of events that ultimately stimulate the production of proteins called **growth factors**. These factors act on prostate tissue to cause the enlargement known as BPH. Studies have shown that BPH tissue has more growth factors than normal prostatic tissue.

Q: Does genetics play a role?

A: Not in the hereditary sense you may have in mind. In fact, there's no strong evidence that BPH runs in families.

However, some researchers think BPH may develop as a result of genetic programming—"instructions" given to cells early in life. In this theory, BPH occurs because cells in one section of the gland follow these instructions and "reawaken" later in life. These "reawakened" cells then deliver signals to other cells in the gland, instructing them to grow or making them more sensitive to hormones that influence growth.

Q: Besides testosterone, are there other hormones that cause BPH?

A: It's believed that estrogen may also play a role. Men's bodies normally make a certain amount of estrogen as well as testosterone, and both sets of hormones stimulate normal prostate tissue. As men age, they produce less testosterone and relatively more estrogen. Studies done with animals suggest that the higher amounts of estrogen in the prostates of older men increase the activity of substances that make the cells grow.

Q: Are there any other theories to explain BPH?

A: Some scientists believe that, in addition to hormonal factors, the nervous system is sending messages to tighten up the prostate's muscle tone. And that means increased pressure on the urethra.

Here's how. As much as 60 percent of the prostatic tissue in people with BPH is **stromal**—that is, tissue that makes up the framework of the gland—and a substantial portion of stromal tissue is made up of muscle. Under an electron microscope, this tissue appears to have larger cells than the prostatic tissue of men who don't have BPH.

Some scientists believe that receptors in the stromal tissue respond to signals from the nervous system and heighten prostatic muscle tone. One group of researchers has suggested that as much as 40 percent of the urethral closure pressure in men with BPH is due to stimulation of prostatic muscles.

Q: Is there anything I can do to prevent getting BPH?

A: Apart from testosterone, researchers haven't identified any special risk factors in men who eventually develop BPH. They can't blame the usual suspects, like smoking, caffeine or obesity. Sexual habits and previous infections don't seem to make any difference. About the only practice that has been clearly implicated in the development of BPH is the use of anabolic steroids by athletes and others who are active in bodybuilding.

One study did find that the risk of BPH seemed to decrease among men who drank between two and four beers a day. Before you head out for a six-pack, however, you should be aware that there's no clear cause and effect. Because men who'd had surgery for BPH were studied, it's possible that they'd changed their drinking habits and were describing their postoperative drinking. Or drinking may correspond to other factors, such as diet.

Q: Does diet have an impact?

A: There are no hard data to say it does. However, it's worth noting that the incidence of BPH among Asian men has historically been very low, and has risen significantly when the men moved to the West or changed their traditional lifestyles. Since Asians tend to have a low-cholesterol, low-fat diet, American men who want to avoid BPH (not to mention heart disease and other health problems) might follow their example.

Q: Is there anything I can do to get rid of BPH?

A: You can't get rid of it any more than you can prevent it. But there are lots of measures you can take to ease urinary difficulties and slow the progress of the disease. You should cut down on fluids in the evening, especially alcohol and caffeine, which stimulate urination. You should urinate frequently; if you overtax your bladder, you'll only aggravate the symptoms. Take your time urinating; allow several minutes to empty the bladder as completely as possible.

You should also be aware that certain prescription drugs can aggravate urinary problems. These include some antispasmodics, including oral bronchodilators, diuretics, tranquilizers and antidepressants. If you're currently taking such medication and you're at an age when you're likely to develop BPH or already have symptoms, you might want to ask your doctor about reducing the dosage or switching to another drug.

There are also some over-the-counter cold remedies, like antihistamines and decongestants, that can worsen a urinary condition. We discuss them later in this section.

Q: What are the symptoms of BPH?

A: There are a number of symptoms associated with BPH. Generally they arise at different stages of the condition. But even if your prostate enlarges to the point where you need to seek surgical or other treatment, you won't necessarily have all of the symptoms. And even if you have all of these symptoms, you don't necessarily have BPH.

Now that you're forewarned, here's a list of what you can expect:

- Urinating more frequently, especially at night
- Some difficulty beginning urination

- A stream that's weak and thin
- Difficulty stopping urination abruptly, often followed by a persistent "dribbling"
- A feeling that you need to urinate urgently
- A feeling that your bladder hasn't completely emptied
- Urinary retention (inability to urinate).

Q: How would I realize that my prostate is growing?

A: You wouldn't, for a while. The condition develops so gradually that it's generally years before you realize there's a problem.

Initially, the bladder compensates for the narrowed urethra by contracting more forcefully than before to push urine through. To do this, the bladder muscle—like any muscle that has to work overtime—thickens, particularly just inside the bladder neck and on the floor of the bladder.

As long as the bladder muscle can overcome the resistance put up by the growing prostate and narrowed urethra, the bladder can empty itself every time you go to the bathroom. In this condition, your bladder is said to be **compensated**, and you don't have any symptoms of BPH.

Q: When do the symptoms set in?

A: Over months and years. As the bladder muscle builds and thickens, the floor of the bladder becomes more sensitive to the presence of urine. The result is that you feel the need to urinate more often. Most men notice this initially at night, when they're awakened by the need to go to the bathroom, so the symptom is called **nocturia**.

As a rule, your bladder can accommodate about five ounces of urine before you feel the need to void. When you're sleeping, you can generally tolerate even more than that without waking up. Furthermore, when you're asleep, the amount of urine your kidneys produce—generally about two ounces each hour when you're awake—falls off. That's why most people can sleep a full eight hours without going to the bathroom.

Once nocturia begins, however, considerably less than five ounces will sound nature's call. As the bladder grows more and more sensitive, you'll wake up once, twice, five times a night.

Q: Why just at night? Why doesn't this happen during the day?

A: You'll probably feel the need to urinate more frequently during the day, too. But that's a feeling people can ignore more easily when they're up and about. It's when you're sleeping, even when you're dreaming, that your brain pays prompt attention.

Q: When I am likely to notice the condition during the day?

A: Probably when your bladder can no longer push effectively past the obstructing prostate. Because the bladder muscle is straining against the resistance of the prostate, you'll start noticing that it takes several seconds to a couple of minutes for your urine flow to start. When the stream finally starts, it's "hesitant" and weak. This condition is called **hesitancy**.

You're particularly likely to run into this situation if you've waited a long time to urinate. Maybe you've been on a long car trip, or refused to budge from your seat during an especially riveting football game. Your bladder may become overstretched and, since it's gradually lost its tone, it contracts only weakly.

Q: How is the bladder affected by all that muscle buildup and stretching?

A: When your bladder starts building muscle, bands of scar tissue, called **trabeculations**, eventually begin to form in the bladder wall. In more advanced cases of BPH, weaker areas of the bladder wall between the areas of trabeculation begin to bulge outward, creating little sacs or pouches called **cellules**.

Eventually the cellules balloon and form small pouches, called **diverticula**, that can trap urine and become a home for bacteria. If you've developed trabeculations and diverticula, you may still have urinary problems even after you've been treated for BPH.

That's also true if your bladder muscle has deteriorated to the point where it's permanently weakened. In that case, you can expect to continue to have a problem with urinary retention.

Q: What happens when the bladder muscle starts to weaken?

A: An annoying phenomenon that doctors call **intermittency** and most men refer to as dribbling. As the obstruction grows, your bladder eventually can't empty itself completely with a single muscle contraction. Your stream of urine stops before your bladder is empty. Seconds later, the muscle contracts a second time, weakly, and the stream starts again.

Sometimes this occurs near the end of the stream. You think you're through urinating, so you zip up. Then anything between a few drops and an ounce or more may dribble onto your underwear.

Q: But at least the bladder is empty, right?

A: Yes. Eventually, however, the bladder becomes **decompensated**. It can't empty, even with a second contraction, so some residual urine is always present. (Under normal conditions, a bladder empties itself almost completely.)

Once the residual urine in the bladder reaches three or four ounces, you notice that it's only a short time after voiding that you feel the need to void again. You may be voiding every 30 minutes to two hours.

As the residual urine builds up to a pint or more, there's no room left in the bladder for new urine coming down from the kidneys, and urine involuntarily leaks from the urethra, usually when you're asleep. This is an advanced stage of BPH.

Q: Are there any symptoms of residual urine?

A: As we just explained, only a short time after urinating, you'll feel the need to urinate again. You may be going to the bathroom as often as every half hour.

You may also become unusually susceptible to bladder or kidney infections. The collecting urine is stagnant, so it's a perfect culture for growing bacteria. If this happens, you begin to feel burning pain when urinating. Often your urine acquires what some people call a barnyard smell.

In addition, some men develop bladder stones. Sometimes they're extremely painful, and sometimes so insignificant they aren't bothersome at all.

Q: Isn't it uncomfortable having all that urine in the bladder?

A: Uncomfortable, and potentially dangerous. If urine can't leave the bladder through the urethra, eventually **reflux** pressure backs the urine into the kidneys. That makes it impossible for the kidneys, which should be filtering and removing various waste products from the body, to do their job. The condition can result in kidney damage and, more rarely still, kidney failure. A condition called **uremic poisoning** can result, which, untreated, can lead to coma and death.

Q: How can I prevent that from happening?

A: Doctors recommend that all men with BPH get a blood test as part of their yearly checkups, to determine how well their kidneys are functioning. The test reveals your levels of **creatinine** and **urea nitrogen**, two of the waste products that the kidneys are supposed to flush constantly out of your blood. If the creatinine level is abnormally high—and that's not unusual if you've had a major problem with residual urine for a long time— that usually means the kidneys have already been damaged.

Q: If my kidneys remain okay, can I live with the condition of urinary retention?

A: If the condition isn't too severe, some men can live that way indefinitely. But other men eventually arrive at a painful state called **acute urinary retention**. That's when they're completely unable to urinate.

Q: What triggers acute urinary retention?

A: It can be brought on suddenly in men with only moderate BPH who take over-the-counter cold remedies or allergy medicines. Antihistamines block nerve impulses. Other medications contain a decongestant drug, known as a **sympathomimetic**, which may, as a side effect, tighten the bladder neck and make it difficult to urinate. (These medications don't usually have this effect on younger people.)

When there's a partial obstruction, urinary retention can also be brought on by alcohol, cold temperatures or a long period of immobility, like being confined to a bed or wheelchair or simply sitting for several hours.

Q: How is acute urinary retention treated?

A: You run—or, more likely, hobble—to your doctor's office or to the emergency department of a hospital. The condition can be alleviated easily and quickly enough; a doctor inserts a catheter into the penis to drain the urine directly from the bladder. Relief is immediate. If you haven't urinated for 12 hours or more, as much as four quarts of urine may pour out.

Q: So acute urinary retention is sudden but somewhat predictable, right? It wouldn't take me by surprise, would it?

A: It's hard to believe, but very occasionally a man may not be aware he has an obstruction until it becomes completely impossible for him to urinate. This condition—the combination of acute urinary retention and asymptomatic obstruction—is called **silent prostatism**.

For several days before the crisis develops, as the man's kidneys fail, he may become extremely weak, sleepy and irritable. Without warning, he may suddenly become comatose. Unless he has his bladder drained immediately, he can die.

Q: How is it possible to have an obstruction and not know it?

A: One explanation is that BPH can develop so gradually that you can get used to the symptoms to the point where you can't remember when you didn't have them. Or maybe you're denying the problem because you don't want anybody tinkering with that part of your anatomy.

Q: Are there any other symptoms of BPH? What about blood in the urine?

A: That's a common symptom. In fact, BPH and bladder cancer are the two most common causes of hematuria in men over 40. You can develop hematuria when the urethral blood vessels and the bladder neck get stretched so much by the growing prostate tissue that they burst.

If it's a very small blood vessel that ruptures, there may be only a microscopic trace of blood in the urine. But if it's a larger blood vessel, the urine will turn pink or red. It's rare but possible for a severe hemorrhage to take place. When that happens, you've got to take care of the condition immediately.

Q: Aren't there lots of urinary problems that people, especially older people, get that aren't due to BPH?

A: You're absolutely right. All the symptoms we've listed above, particularly residual urine, often occur in elderly women. Obviously, you can't blame the prostate for that.

The symptoms that are characteristic of BPH can also be caused by urethral **stricture** or scarring, bladder problems, inflammation, infection or other conditions, such as neurological disorders.

Diabetes can lead to frequent urination and can interfere with sexual performance. It's not unusual for a man to think he has prostate problems when he's really showing signs of diabetes. The same problems can also be caused by some of those medications we mentioned earlier, like antihistamines or decongestants, that can interfere with bladder function.

Q: So if I have urinary problems, how do I know it's due to BPH?

A: If there's a possibility that you have any of the conditions we just mentioned, and particularly if you're under 55, you should have a series of diagnostic tests to determine bladder function. According to several studies, about one-third of men who are told that their incontinence is due to prostate enlargement actually learn from **urodynamic studies** that there's an altogether different cause.

Q: How do doctors determine that it's BPH?

A: A number of ways. They start by taking a history that includes information about your sexual habits. They want to know, for example, whether you've ever had a venereal infection, which can result in symptoms similar to those seen in prostate disorders. They also want to know how often you urinate and whether there's been any change in the pattern.

Because it's hard to give more than a subjective account, you can help the diagnostic process by monitoring your urinary habits before the visit. On a sheet of paper, write down about four urinary habits. (You can take any of the several symptoms we enumerated earlier.) Each day, put a check for each time the problem occurs. After one week, you'll have a factual record to present to the doctor.

Q: What about a physical exam—how would it help diagnose BPH?

A: In such an exam the doctor may press down on your bladder to determine whether it's full of urine and distended. He's also likely to do a rectal exam, though that's of limited use in detecting BPH. The rectal exam indicates whether the prostate is enlarged. However, the part of the prostate that generally causes obstruction is the middle lobe, or central zone, since that's what tightens around the urethra. Unfortunately, that's the part that can never be felt during a rectal exam.

Q: But shouldn't the size of the prostate overall indicate whether I'm developing BPH?

A: Not necessarily. As a rule, the size of the prostate doesn't reflect how severe the obstruction is. Some men with greatly enlarged prostates have little obstruction and few symptoms, while others, whose glands are less enlarged, have more blockage and greater problems.

Q: Are there diagnostic tests that tell more?

A: The doctor will probably do a urinalysis and urine culture, to look for infection. The presence of red blood cells suggests problems in the urinary tract, such as stones or tumors, but it may also indicate BPH. White blood cells or pus may indicate infection or inflammation in the kidneys, **ureters** or bladder.

He may also conduct a urodynamic evaluation, which may consist of a urine flow test and a residual urine test. To measure urine flow, he'll use either a machine called a **uroflometer**, or just a stopwatch and a measuring container; you'll contribute a full bladder. The doctor will measure what you think is your strongest flow, and compare it with the standard flow rate for your age-group. Men over 60 should have a flow rate greater than 13 milliliters per second, for example, compared with 22 milliliters per second for men under 40.

Q: Is that proof of BPH?

A: No. A slow flow rate may sometimes be due to a weak bladder muscle, not to prostate problems. Other tests are necessary.

Q: What about the test for residual urine?

A: That's done with a **bladder catheterization**.
After you've emptied your bladder (or think you have), the doctor inserts a catheter into the bladder for a few minutes to measure the amount of residual urine. In theory, the more residual urine, the greater the need for treatment of the obstruction. However, residual urine can also indicate a weak bladder muscle.

Q: I've heard of a **Foley catheter.** Is that what's used?

A: No. When the doctor is merely measuring residual urine, he uses a simple "in-and-out" catheter. A Foley catheter is designed to be left in the bladder for long periods of time and stays inside with the help of an inflatable bag that catches on the bladder neck.

There are many different reasons for using Foley catheters but, in the case of BPH, they're normally inserted when the prostate is so large that a man can't urinate at all. As a rule, the catheter remains only until the problem of the obstruction is resolved. But the catheter may remain indefinitely if the patient refuses to be treated or his medical condition is so bad that he's considered a poor risk for surgery.

Q: Are there blood tests used to diagnose BPH?

A: While there aren't any blood studies that diagnose BPH, you can expect some blood tests during the exam, and certainly before any surgery takes place.

We've already mentioned those blood tests for kidney function. There are two other blood tests, for **prostatic**

acid phosphatase (PAP) and prostate-specific antigen (PSA) levels, that are routinely performed on men being examined for BPH. However, the primary purpose of both these tests is to detect prostate cancer.

We describe these tests at greater length in the final section of this chapter. Let us just say here that the results of the PSA test must be handled with care. Men with enlarged prostates tend to get elevated PSA readings, which can also indicate the presence of prostate cancer. So if you have a high PSA level, you may be subjected to other tests —and a lot of worry—until it can be determined that the only problem is BPH.

Q: What about x-rays?

A: Some urologists take an **excretory urogram**, also known as an **intravenous pyelogram (IVP)** or **intravenous urogram (IVU)**, which provides a lot of information about the entire urinary tract. It's performed by injecting (into a vein in the forearm) a dye that concentrates in the kidneys and appears white against the dark background of an x-ray.

The dye's passage through the system over the course of half an hour is recorded on a series of films. It shows how well a patient empties his bladder, shows any obstruction to the drainage of the kidneys and even indicates the size of the prostate, through a shadow it casts within the bladder.

However, there's a major drawback to IVPs. People have had serious—and occasionally even fatal—allergic reactions to the dye. One explanation may be that iodine is the base of some of the injected material. It's almost impossible to predict who may have a bad reaction, so an alternative dye has been developed. But it's extremely expensive. Many urologists prefer to use other tests.

Q: What other tests might be done if I'm being examined or treated for BPH?

A: **Renal scans**, produced after injecting a very small amount of radioactive material, give a picture of the kidneys. So does **ultrasound**, a totally noninvasive procedure that is generally considered one of the safest tests. But while ultrasound can help estimate the size of the prostate, to determine the best surgical approach, it doesn't help you or your doctor decide whether surgery or other treatment is actually needed. That's because prostate size isn't an indication of the extent of obstruction.

Q: Is there anything else I need to know about testing and diagnosing BPH?

A: While none of the tests and examinations we've described is conclusive alone, as a group they can confirm a diagnosis of BPH. But as we said in the first chapter, cystoscopy is extremely useful in diagnosing every prostatic disease, and BPH is no exception.

A cystoscope lets a doctor see the degree of obstruction in the prostatic urethra, estimate the size and weight of the obstructing prostatic tissue, and determine how best to approach it surgically. She'll also be able to measure any residual urine that may be present, since the urine will come out through the cystoscope after it has entered the bladder. And it shows changes in the bladder, such as the trabeculations we spoke of earlier.

But it cannot say whether you actually need treatment for BPH—that is, whether the obstruction is bothersome. That's up to you.

Q: If I've got BPH, does that increase my chances of having prostatic cancer, too?

A: It's true that the two often appear together, but that's only because both diseases are fairly common in older men. Men with enlarged prostates subsequently develop cancer no more often than do men with normal-size glands.

When men have surgery for BPH, a procedure we describe in the next chapter, the tissue removed is routinely checked for hidden cancer cells. In about 1 out of 10 cases, some cancer tissue is found. Often, however, it's limited to a few cells of a nonaggressive type of cancer, and no treatment is needed. Although BPH and prostate cancer share many of the same symptoms, having BPH doesn't seem to increase the likelihood that you'll get prostate cancer.

PROSTATE CANCER

Q: What is prostate cancer?

A: Cancer of the prostate is almost always a primary cancer, meaning that it originates in the prostate, rather than traveling there from another part of the body. Typically it begins in the outer part of the prostate. As the tumor grows, it may spread to the inner part of the prostate. Like other cancers, prostate cancer can then **metastasize**, or spread, to other parts of the body.

In many cases, however, prostatic cancer is a very slow-growing malignancy. Autopsy studies have shown that about one-third of men over the age of 50 have microscopic evidence of prostate cancer, yet the vast majority of these cancers grow so slowly they never become a threat to life. Hence the common statement that "most men die *with* prostate cancer, not *of* it."

Q: Who gets prostate cancer?

A: In hard numbers, approximately one in every nine men develops prostate cancer at some time in his life. (As a point of comparison, a woman's lifetime risk of developing breast cancer is also one in nine.) In 1992, the American Cancer Society (ACS) estimated that 165,000 new prostate cancers would be diagnosed during 1993, and 35,000 men would die of the disease.

And the numbers are going up, largely due to improved detection. Since the 1980s, incidence of prostate cancer has risen 4 percent a year. It's increasing faster than any other cancer, except skin cancer. If you count out skin cancers, prostate cancer is now the most common cancer in American men. It accounts for about 11 percent of cancer deaths in men, a distant second to lung cancer.

Q: If it's almost as common as breast cancer, why haven't I heard more about it?

A: One reason is that, because prostate cancer can be difficult to detect, it's been significantly underreported. Another factor is that, until quite recently, well-known men who developed prostate cancer have declined to go public. Although Cornelius Ryan, author of such bestsellers as *A Bridge Too Far,* wrote a book about his experience with prostate cancer, it's noteworthy that it was called *A Private Battle* (and it was published posthumously).

No doubt you remember that breast cancer, too, was a little-discussed disease until people of the stature of Betty Ford, the former First Lady, began to talk openly about their diagnoses and treatments.

Men are paying a price for their reticence. Although money for research doesn't necessarily buy results, it's interesting that, in fiscal 1993, the National Cancer Institute (NCI) budgeted some $37 million for prostate-

cancer research, compared with $197 million for
breast cancer.

Q: Wait a minute. Wasn't there some well-known
public figure who "went public" with
the disease?

A: It's true that lately prostate cancer has been
emerging in the headlines. You are probably
thinking of Senate Minority Leader Bob Dole, who talked
about his 1991 surgery for prostate cancer and urged
other men to "be on the lookout for this stuff." Other
prominent men have since announced that they're being
treated for the disease; for some, it's been given as the
cause of death in obituaries.

Q: Why are there so many new diagnoses of
prostate cancer?

A: The main reason, apart from the aging of the popu-
lation, is the growing number of prostatectomies
—operations to reduce enlarged prostates. Routine analysis
of the prostatic "chips" that are removed during the
surgery allows doctors to detect prostate cancer at a very
early stage, and that adds to the statistics.

Q: But is prostate cancer actually occurring
more often?

A: Some NCI researchers, who have analyzed mortality
trends and laboratory studies of certain prostate
tumors, say that part of the increase could reflect changes
in the real risk of prostatic cancer. But nobody knows
why prostate cancer should be on the rise, except that
overall cancer incidence is rising, according to the NCI.

Q: If I've had a prostatectomy for BPH, how can I get cancer?

A: As we discuss in detail in Chapter 3, a partial prostatectomy for BPH removes the new tissue but leaves the original prostate intact. So, unfortunately, it's as capable of developing cancer as a prostate that's never been touched.

Q: Who's at risk for getting prostate cancer?

A: The main risk factor is age. The older you are, the greater your chances of developing prostate cancer. That one-in-nine incidence is for men throughout their lives; it's a rarity in young men, and risk rises steadily with age. More than 80 percent of prostate tumors are diagnosed in men age 65 or more. Autopsy studies have found evidence of prostate cancer in 70 percent of men who were 80 or older who died of unrelated causes.

Q: But are some men more likely to get it than others?

A: Definitely. Much like female breast cancer, prostate cancer runs in families. The American Medical Association has estimated that a man whose father or brother had prostate cancer—particularly if the relative was under 65—has about twice the usual risk. NCI's Division of Cancer Prevention and Control has said epidemiological data—statistics on the incidence of disease—show that men who have more than one relative with prostate cancer may have up to six times the average risk.

The other high-risk group is African-American men. According to the ACS, they have the highest rate of prostate cancer in the world. They also have double the mortality rate for men with prostate cancer, though that statistic may reflect their access to medical care rather than physiological factors.

Some researchers think, however, that race isn't nearly as critical a factor as diet, which we discuss later in this section. H. Ballentine Carter of the Johns Hopkins University School of Medicine, in Baltimore, cites epidemiological data indicating that black men living in Africa have among the lowest rates of prostate cancer in the world, but when they emigrate to the United States, their risk of developing prostate cancer increases tenfold. There are similar findings about Asians who emigrate to this country and abandon their traditional low-fat diets.

Q: I've read that **vasectomies** can lead to prostate cancer. True?

A: Two recent studies, conducted by a team headed by Edward Giovannucci, M.D., from Brigham and Women's Hospital and Harvard University, in Boston, have reported that a vasectomy appears to increase significantly a man's risk of developing prostate cancer. They also found that, the more time that had passed since a vasectomy, the greater the man's risk of developing cancer.

One study found that men who'd had vasectomies were, overall, 66 percent likelier to develop prostate cancer than men who hadn't. The other study found that men who'd had a vasectomy more than 20 years earlier faced up to an 89 percent greater risk of prostate cancer than men who hadn't had vasectomies.

Q: Why should a vasectomy raise the risk of cancer?

A: No one really knows, and it's highly possible that there's no cause-and-effect. Previous studies have failed to find any relationship.

Q: **Should I have my vasectomy reversed?**

A: The *Journal of the American Medical Association,* which published the studies, editorialized that "the data are far too preliminary to consider vasectomy reversal to reduce the risk of prostate cancer." It said men who have had vasectomies should follow American Cancer Society guidelines for regular screenings, which we detail elsewhere in this chapter.

Q: **What actually causes prostate cancer?**

A: Both epidemiological studies and laboratory research have shown a clear connection between prostate cancer and androgens, or male hormones, especially testosterone. Numerous other studies have also suggested a connection between a high-fat diet and high levels of testosterone.

Men who have higher testosterone levels seem to have a higher rate of prostate cancer. African-Americans, for example, have slightly higher levels of testosterone than white American men. Interestingly, autopsy studies have found that men around the world have a similar incidence of latent carcinoma, or slow-growing microscopic cancers. But in countries where people eat more fat and have higher testosterone levels, these tumors are likely to blossom into full-blown cancer that is more aggressive— meaning that it spreads and is difficult to cure.

Some men who develop prostate cancer undergo treatment in which their testosterone is removed, either surgically or through hormonal therapy. As a rule, their tumors regress, for months or even years. Although the testosterone is gone, eventually the tumors do recur. No one fully understands how testosterone can lead to prostatic cancer, or how tumors can recur without it.

Staging Prostate Cancer

Q: How does prostate cancer spread?

A: Before answering, we should note that many prostate cancers never spread; they remain completely localized within the prostatic capsule. If and when a tumor does metastasize, it moves initially to the neighboring organs. Eventually it may also travel to the bone, lungs, chest and even brain.

When it is diagnosed, each tumor is classified into a specific stage, based on its size, extent, location and microscopic appearance. Over time, the tumor may progress through a handful of stages.

Q: What are the stages?

A: There are several systems for grading prostate cancer, all based on what the tumor looks like and how it behaves. The most common system uses four stages of prostate cancer, A, B, C and D. There are subclassifications within stages A, B and D.

Q: I suppose stage A is the earliest-stage tumor?

A: That's right. Stage A cancer is found incidentally, in tissue that's removed from enlarged prostates. It's too early to turn up on a rectal exam or any other screening test. It's a peculiar tumor; in some men, it can be latent for decades, while in others it can advance so aggressively that it kills within a year or two. Usually, but not always, it's confined to the prostate. These cancers are usually subdivided into the less malignant stage A1 and the more malignant stage A2.

Q: How is stage B cancer detected?

A: It's typically found during a routine rectal exam, when the doctor feels a hard or firm area of the prostate. The man himself is probably unaware there's a problem, because the cancer at this stage is contained within the prostate and not causing any symptoms. If the tumor is small, it's considered a stage B1 cancer; if it's larger, it moves up to B2.

Q: If I have stage C cancer, do I know it?

A: Probably not. Stage C cancer is more advanced and larger than A or B, but the cancer is confined within the prostatic capsule and there still aren't any symptoms. It may be detected by rectal exam, in which most of the prostate is hard or firm and filled with cancer. However, the cancer may also have extended beyond the bladder into the seminal vesicles.

Q: And stage D is in the bones?

A: That's the final stage. Stage D cancer has spread outside the prostate. If it's spread immediately outside, or to pelvic **lymph nodes** near the prostate, it's stage D1. If the cancer has spread far from the prostate to, say, the lungs, the bones or the liver, it's stage D2.

Q: When prostate cancer is first diagnosed, what percentage is usually A, B and so on?

A: There aren't any hard numbers. And even if there were, it might not be all that meaningful. Because the diagnostic process leaves much to be desired, as we discuss below, there's been a tendency over the years to understage prostate cancer—that is, to underestimate how far it's spread.

Having said that, we can say that experts estimate that between 30 and 50 percent of prostate cancers are already at stage D when they're first diagnosed. Repeated surveys by the American College of Surgeons show that more than 40 percent of newly diagnosed prostate cancers have already spread beyond the prostate, and that this overall pattern has remained virtually unchanged for years.

Q: Can prostate cancer be cured?

A: As with any cancer, that depends on what stage it has reached. It also depends on your definition of the word "cure."

The vast majority of men whose tumors are still confined to the prostate when they're diagnosed live as long as men who never get prostate cancer.

If the cancer has escaped the prostatic capsule, the survival rate over the next five years falls to about 45 percent. And if it has spread to the lymph nodes or bone, or through the bloodstream to other organs, like the liver or bladder, the survival rate drops to 15 to 20 percent.

For a great many men, slowing the cancer's inexorable progress is as significant an aspect of treatment as destroying it when it's still vulnerable. In Chapter 4, we discuss the various treatments for prostate cancer, including the no-treatment option.

Diagnosing Prostate Cancer

Q: What are the symptoms of prostate cancer?

A: Unfortunately, most prostate cancers are "silent," which is to say they don't cause noticeable symptoms or problems for months or even years. The cancer must grow fairly large before it presses on the urethra and causes trouble with urination. Symptoms of more advanced prostate cancer include blood in the urine, urinating at night, pain on urination, or any sudden change in normal urinary habits.

Q: Wait a minute! Those are the same symptoms you said characterize BPH. What's the difference?

A: The main difference is that, if you have BPH, the symptoms develop gradually. With cancer, they may begin quite abruptly.

And prostate cancer may produce a few symptoms not normally associated with BPH. Ejaculation may become painful. And since prostate cancer is the leading cause of bone metastases, which may cause back pain, unexplained back pain can also be a sign. The pain is usually in the spine, but it may also be in the bony pelvis, the lower back, the hips, or the bones of the upper legs.

Q: So the lack of symptoms makes it hard to detect prostate cancer before it has spread?

A: That's part of the problem. Another part, according to the medical establishment, is that men don't show up dutifully for their annual rectal exams. But even if they did, it might not be worth the trip.

Q: What do you mean?

A: The results of early-detection programs have been so disappointing, in terms of finding curable tumors, that some leading members of the medical community have wondered whether mass screening is worthwhile. In a comprehensive review in *Ca—A Cancer Journal for Clinicians,* published by the ACS, three researchers took a long, hard look at some of the statistics to date, and conclude that there is "no clear evidence to suggest decreased mortality from any diagnostic test."

Q: Meaning that none of the measures used to diagnose prostate cancer saves lives?

A: Unfortunately, that's right. But that situation may be changing, thanks to a handful of new tests and some new technology. There are three screening methods that, not alone but in various combinations, are generating a lot of interest in the medical community: the rectal exam, the prostate-specific antigen (PSA) test, and **transrectal ultrasound**.

Let's discuss them one at a time, starting with that old standby, so to speak: the rectal exam.

Rectal Exams

Q: How effective are rectal exams?

A: The traditional view has been that rectal exams are a highly reliable means of catching most prostate cancers before they spread. Unfortunately, there's a growing body of evidence to the contrary. Studies have shown that most patients have advanced disease by the time they're diagnosed by rectal exam. An analysis of the medical records of a large health maintenance organization in California, published in *Lancet* in 1991, concludes that "screening by routine digital rectal examination appears to have little if any effect in preventing metastatic prostatic cancer."

A recent clinical study was even more devastating to the traditional view. In this study, an annual rectal exam detected prostate cancer in 56 men—38 men in the first exam, 18 men the following year. Six years later, six of the men who were diagnosed during the second rectal exam had died of prostate cancer. That works out to an exceedingly high mortality rate of 33 percent—compared with only 8 percent of the men whose cancer was detected during the initial exam.

Q: Why would a competent rectal exam fail to detect cancer?

A: Several studies have suggested that tumors that are small and confined to the prostate may be hard to detect by rectal exam. One major reason is that many of the cancers start on the far side of the prostate, opposite the rectum, so they cannot be felt. The authors of the clinical study theorize that the tumors found in the second group were more aggressive and grew faster—hence the higher mortality rate.

Q: Then what's the answer—monthly rectal exams?

A: Not quite, but the researchers did suggest that the rectal exam might be performed more frequently than once a year. However, given the high dropout rate in their own study, in which the exam was free, it's doubtful that stepping up the recommended number of digital exams would be very effective. An alternative, the researchers say, is that a more sensitive test may be required to detect these tumors when they're still curable.

Prostate-Specific Antigen (PSA) Test

Q: What about the PSA test? How does that detect tumors?

A: Prostate-specific antigen is a glycoprotein enzyme produced almost exclusively by the prostate and detectable in all men who have prostates and normal levels of testosterone. However, the level of the enzyme rises in men with prostate cancer. Studies have found that, gram for gram, the average prostate cancer produces at least 10 times the amount of PSA produced by normal prostatic tissue.

Q: How are results measured?

A: PSA levels, taken from blood samples, are stated in terms of nanograms, or billionths of a gram, per milliliter. A normal PSA level would be less than 4 ng/ml. A PSA level between 4 and 10 ng/ml is in the "gray area" that may indicate a local tumor. A level above 10 points strongly to cancer, and possibly to metastasis.

Q: How does the PSA test compare with a rectal exam?

A: Favorably, overall. In one major study involving 150,000 men, PSA was twice as accurate as the rectal exam in finding cancer. PSA accurately predicted cancer 40 percent of the time, while a positive rectal exam was correct only 20 percent of the time.

Q: So the PSA test can detect cancer before there's a palpable lump in the prostate?

A: There's some indication that PSA levels start to rise, within the normal range, as many as 10 years before a tumor is diagnosed. A study at Johns Hopkins University, using stored serum, found a connection between small annual increases in PSA levels and a subsequent diagnosis of prostate cancer. While PSA levels tend to rise as men age, the rate of change was significantly greater in men who would eventually be diagnosed with prostate cancer.

Q: It sounds like PSA is sensitive enough to be a good diagnostic tool for prostate cancer. True?

A: It's sensitive, all right—so sensitive, as we indicated in the previous section, that it's highly controversial.

There are two major problems with the PSA test. The first is that it may give you the wrong answer. The other is that it may tell you more than you need to know.

Q: What do you mean—give me the wrong answer?

A: PSA test results are often false negatives—that is, they're normal even if cancer is present. In studies, between 20 and 40 percent of men with localized prostatic cancers had normal PSA levels. False-positive results, or high levels of PSA when there's no cancer, are also common.

A number of extraneous factors can result in false positives. If you have prostatitis, for example, your PSA level rises temporarily. A major trauma or injury to your prostate, such as an operation or biopsy, can increase your PSA level fiftyfold and keep it there for two weeks. (Research indicates, however, that a rectal exam has only a negligible effect on PSA levels.)

But the main reason for false positives is the growth of benign prostatic tissue. An enlarged prostate produces more prostate-specific antigen. And since BPH is so common in the same age-group that's at risk for prostate cancer, many in the medical community consider the PSA test unreliable for diagnosing prostate cancer.

Q: So it's impossible to obtain a reliable PSA reading when the prostate's enlarged?

A: One scientist claims he's found a way to correct for BPH. Fred Lee, M.D., director of the Prostate Center at Crittenton Hospital, in Rochester, Michigan, has developed a formula that correlates PSA levels with prostate size. If the prostate is enlarged, Lee's formula predicts a higher-than-normal PSA level. "We determine how large the gland is and we predict how much PSA the man is entitled to," Lee says. It's only if the test level is appreciably higher that cancer is suspected.

But to use this technique, Lee cautions, the man should do nothing that would reduce the size of his prostate, and thus throw off the calculations, before its volume is determined by ultrasound and his PSA is measured. That means no biopsies or medications that would make the prostate smaller.

Q:

You also said the PSA test may tell me more than I need to know. What do you mean?

A:

A critical issue is whether an early finding of cancer increases a man's life span or just his anxiety level. For older men with prostate cancer, many doctors believe, ignorance may be bliss. "The PSA test may identify many men with small, slow-growing cancers who will then want to be cured with treatments that may be more destructive than the tumors themselves," says Barry Kramer, M.D., associate director for the National Cancer Institute's Early Detection and Community Oncology Program.

Other doctors argue, however, that men should be informed about the PSA test and then decide what they want to do. Not every older man who learns he has prostate cancer will elect treatment.

Q:

How frequently should I have a PSA test?

A:

The American Cancer Society, while conceding there are "recognized problems" with using PSA as a screen, recommends that all men 50 and over have a PSA test each year along with their rectal exams. Some doctors, like Joseph E. Oesterling, a urologist at the Mayo Clinic, in Rochester, Minnesota, believe that men in the high-risk groups we mentioned earlier, such as men whose fathers or brothers have had prostate cancer, should start annual screenings between ages 40 to 45.

But many who defend the PSA test would stop its use after a certain age. Men with a life expectancy of fewer than 10 years shouldn't undergo the test, says Oesterling, adding, "I see no point in screening an 88-year-old man with heart and lung disease and a short life-expectancy." He takes the same position on rectal exams.

At any rate, the choice is yours. Hundreds of medical centers, with underwriting from drug companies, have leapt onto the PSA bandwagon and are offering free PSA tests to screen for prostate cancer.

Transrectal Ultrasound

Q: What's involved in a transrectal ultrasound?

A: It works like any ultrasound. In this case, the ultrasound is sent out by a probe inserted into the rectum. The waves bounce off the prostate, and a computer uses the echoes to create a picture called a **sonogram**. Most prostate cancers appear less dense than the surrounding tissue.

Q: Is it reliable?

A: There are not much data on the role of ultrasound alone in detecting prostate cancer. And what data exist aren't terribly encouraging.

Preliminary results of the American Cancer Society National Prostate Cancer Detection Project, a multicenter study evaluating the use of all three screening methods in nearly 3,000 men, indicate that ultrasound is sensitive to a fault in detecting cancer. While it detected more tumors than a rectal exam did, it yielded an appalling number of false positives (often in cases of BPH) and missed about one-quarter of the cancers. It also picked up a large number of tumors classified as premalignant that could probably be safely ignored for years, and possibly forever.

Q: Why doesn't ultrasound do a better job of finding tumors?

A: There are a number of reasons. Some tumors simply don't show up well on ultrasound. Conversely, many areas that look like tumors are merely tissue that's inflamed.

Unlike a PSA level, a sonogram's meaning is in the eye of the beholder. When Fred Lee, a veteran radiologist, conducted his own studies of ultrasound as a means of detecting prostate cancer, his results were significantly more impressive. Lee complains that many urologists have acquired ultrasound equipment and are using it as a diagnostic tool, but don't know how to read the sonogram.

Q: What's the effect of combining all three tests to diagnose prostate cancer?

A: Studies indicate that the whole is greater than the sum of the parts—that is, that each test can detect tumors the other two may overlook, eliminate a number of the false-positive results, or at least add more information to the diagnosis. In a preliminary report, researchers on the ACS National Prostate Cancer Detection Project conclude that "it may be possible to increase the early detection of prostate cancer substantially" through a combination of rectal exam, ultrasound and PSA.

However, there's still no ironclad proof that, if you underwent all three tests every year, you'd increase your odds of surviving prostate cancer.

Q: What's the most effective combination of tests?

A: Good question, and one the medical community is asking. So far, nobody has the answer.

One study, in which some 1,700 men were tested, recommended the combination of PSA and rectal exam and, in patients with abnormal findings, ultrasound. But even that study's authors caution that their results hadn't established that such testing would improve survival rates.

In 1993 the NCI launched a 16-year clinical trial, in which 37,000 men, aged 60 to 74, are to be screened with rectal exams and PSA tests for prostate cancer. Positive results for either screen will lead to further diagnostic tests, including transrectal ultrasound. But any definitive answers to the questions about screening, including at what age it should take place and how frequently, are years away.

Biopsy and Other Staging Tests

Q: If one or more of the tests are positive, what's the next step?

A: Usually the doctor performs a biopsy, inserting a needle through the rectum or, sometimes, the perineum, and into the prostate to remove a core of tissue. The tissue is examined under a microscope for cancer cells. Microscopic examination is the only way to make a definitive diagnosis. To determine the extent of the cancer, the doctor may do multiple biopsies to sample a wide area of prostate tissue.

Q: Is biopsy painful?

A: Two recent inventions have made biopsy a relatively painless procedure that can be done without anesthesia. One is a spring-loaded biopsy "gun," which is guided by ultrasound through the rectum to suspicious areas of the prostate. The "gun" works so fast and uses such a fine needle that it's barely perceptible.

The other device is a skinny-needle **aspiration**-type biopsy, in which cells are literally aspirated, or sucked, out of the gland through a very thin needle inserted through the rectum.

Q: Is biopsy safe?

A: It's often presented as an innocuous procedure, but there is one significant risk: Rectal bacteria can easily enter the prostate. Because of this risk, you are given antibiotics before the procedure to ward off infection. Even so, you may get a persistent low-grade prostatitis that, as we discussed earlier in the chapter, can be hard to shake. (Men who already have prostatitis should not have a biopsy, according to Stephen N. Rous, the urologist-author of *The Prostate Book*.) An infection can also increase your PSA level, which makes it difficult to detect cancer in subsequent tests until the infection is finally cleared up.

Q: Who should be biopsied?

A: Anyone who may have prostatic cancer. Given the difficulties in detecting the disease, however, that can be a slightly amorphous category.

Certainly one group would be men whose rectal exams disclose irregularities or lumps. Another group would be men with PSAs above 10 ng/ml. Another would be men with telltale symptoms, like sudden—rather than gradual —trouble urinating, or bone pain, and suspicious x-rays or **bone scans**.

Q: **What if I've got a medium-range PSA? Should I be biopsied?**

A: Increasingly, doctors are automatically ordering biopsies and ultrasounds for men whose PSA levels are between 4 and 10 ng/ml. Some experts thinks that's overreacting. Fred Lee, for example, believes too many biopsies are being done by urologists who don't know how to read ultrasounds. "You don't have to have a biopsy on day one," he advises. "Don't let anyone biopsy you just because your PSA is elevated." He urges men to get an ultrasound that's expertly read and that also measures the size of their prostates.

Q: **What happens if the biopsy is positive for prostate cancer?**

A: The next task is to determine the stage, or extent, of the cancer. Is it contained in the prostatic capsule? Has it spread to the lymph nodes? Is it in the bones? **Staging**, or determining what stage the cancer has reached, is a critical part of the diagnosis because it determines treatment.

Historically, rectal exams were used for staging but, given their dismal record on diagnosis, you won't be surprised to hear that they weren't very accurate. Now there are several blood tests and imaging techniques that are far more effective.

Q: What are the blood tests?

A: The main one is that mixed blessing, the PSA. While it's controversial as a diagnostic technique, it gets more respect as a staging tool. Researchers have found that it's extremely accurate at predicting whether the cancer has reached its final stage: metastasis to bone.

A study at the Mayo Clinic of more than 850 men with newly diagnosed, untreated prostate cancer found that, of 561 men with PSA levels of 10 ng/ml or less and no bone pain, only three had abnormal results on bone scans. Of the 467 men whose PSA level was 8 or less, none had abnormal bone scans. For practical purposes, concluded Joseph Oesterling, the principal author, men with no bone pain and a PSA level below 10 can skip the scan—at a savings, on average, of $600.

Q: Are there other blood tests?

A: If your biopsy is positive, your blood, urine or prostatic secretions will be checked for prostatic acid phosphatase (PAP) levels. PAP is generally elevated in men with spreading prostate cancer.

Q: So a high PAP level means I have metastatic prostate cancer?

A: Not necessarily. There are a number of other conditions that can raise the level: BPH, prostatitis, Paget's disease (a bone disorder), pneumonia and hepatitis. Atromid-S, a drug taken to lower cholesterol levels in the blood, can have the same effect. Even a rectal exam and prostatic massage, which we described earlier, can raise PAP levels.

Q: How can a rectal exam affect PAP levels?

A: While PSA is made almost exclusively by the prostate, the enzymes that make PAP can be produced by other body tissues, including the rectum. So when that area gets manipulated during a rectal exam, it may release these enzymes into general circulation and temporarily raise PAP levels.

Q: What other tests are used in staging?

A: You probably will already have had a transrectal ultrasound, as part of either the diagnostic process or the biopsy. But if you haven't, then your doctor most likely will order one after a positive biopsy. He may also order one or two other imaging procedures.

One is a **computerized tomography scan (CT or CAT scan)**, a series of detailed pictures that are created by a computer linked to an x-ray machine. The scan can show whether the lymph nodes are swollen, which might mean the cancer has spread there. The other procedure, **magnetic resonance imaging (MRI)**, links a computer to a powerful magnet, instead of x-rays, to produce pictures of the prostate and nearby lymph nodes. And of course, there's the bone scan.

Q: What does a bone scan show?

A: A bone scan shows whether cancer has spread to the bone. When cancer spreads from prostate to bone, it attacks and partially destroys the bone. The body tries to repair the damage by laying down new bone in the damaged area. A bone scan can reveal that information, months before a standard x-ray shows anything.

Q: How does a bone scan work?

A: A radioactive substance is injected into a vein in your arm, and moves from the blood to the bone. If there are bones under repair because they've been damaged, they absorb the isotope. A counting machine similar to a Geiger counter scans the entire body and tallies the amount of isotope that's taken up by each bone. Each of these counts shows up as a dot on a screen or a monitor. A lot of counts or dots indicates that cancer has spread to that bone.

Q: Is a bone scan accurate?

A: Yes, with one proviso: It isn't designed to show cancer, only bone repair. So a high count can also signal bone fractures or even arthritis. However, if you already have a positive biopsy, a high radioactive count is a pretty strong indication that the cancer has spread. And an x-ray can then show whether the bone looks normal or damaged—as it would be if you had arthritis, for example.

Q: At least there's no surgery involved in staging, right?

A: Sorry, there may be. The only way to tell for sure if the lymph nodes have cancer is to biopsy them. If all the other tests put your cancer in a gray zone, your doctor may want to perform a pelvic **lymphadenectomy**, a biopsy of the lymph nodes surrounding the prostatic area. This is a surgical procedure in which the abdomen is opened and the tissue is removed. It may be analyzed while you're still on the operating table. Sometimes this is done right before a **radical prostatectomy**, an operation we discuss in Chapter 4.

There are two alternatives to the open lymphadenectomy that you may find more acceptable. The least invasive—but also least accurate—is a **lymphangiogram**, in which dye is injected into the lymph system and travels to the pelvic area. At that point, an x-ray can reveal cancer in the nodes. The other, newer approach involves **laparoscopy**, or the use of a small viewing tube to gain access to the interior of the abdomen. In a laparoscopic pelvic dissection, the doctor can remove and examine lymph nodes without the trauma of major surgery. The dissection can be understood, at the outset, to be purely a staging technique and not necessarily a commitment to a prostatectomy.

Prevention

Q: Can prostate cancer be prevented?

A: Unfortunately, we really know very little about ways to prevent prostate cancer. However, a number of epidemiological studies suggest a connection between prostate cancer and diet. A 1982 report by the National Research Council named prostate cancer, along with breast cancer and colon cancer, as the three forms of cancer most strongly linked to dietary factors.

Q: What kinds of foods are linked to prostate cancer?

A: The main culprit is fat, especially animal fat. A number of studies show that men who eat large amounts of animal fats have significantly higher rates of prostate cancer than men who eat relatively little animal fat. There's also evidence that men who eat a lot of animal fat develop a form of prostate cancer that spreads faster and is more difficult to cure.

A study at Loma Linda University, in California, for example, found that male Seventh-day Adventists who ate a lot of fatty foods (such as meat, cheese and eggs) were 3½ times more likely to have fatal prostate cancer than Adventist men who didn't eat those foods very much. (Most Adventists are vegetarians.) Other studies point to an increased risk for heavy milk drinkers, especially when it's whole milk.

Q: How can fat in foods affect the prostate?

A: Some researchers believe that it raises the levels of both testosterone and certain estrogens that stimulate the prostate to grow, along with any cancer cells it may harbor.

Q: So those are the bad foods. Are there foods that are good?

A: The evidence on foods that actually fight prostate cancer is more mixed. Some researchers say there's no apparent link between fruits and vegetables that are rich in vitamins A and C and a lower incidence of prostate cancer.

But other studies suggest that a diet of grains, legumes, fruits and vegetables can help prevent prostate cancer. A study of some 750 men by Roswell Park Memorial Institute, in Buffalo, New York, found that a diet with a lot of **beta-carotene** seemed to lower the risk for men who were under 69 years of age (but didn't affect older men). Beta-carotene is found in dark-green leafy vegetables like broccoli and spinach, and in deep yellow and orange vegetables and fruits like carrots and cantaloupe, as well as in vitamin supplements.

Q: Are there any other vitamins that are helpful?

A: Lately some researchers have hypothesized that vitamin D may also be effective against prostate cancer. It's found in vitamin D-enriched milk, fish liver oil, salmon, tuna, sardines, egg yolks and margarine, and in vitamin supplements. Of course, the major source of vitamin D is sunlight.

Q: So sunlight can fight prostate cancer?

A: That's still only a hunch, but an interesting one at that. Published in 1992, a study by researchers at the University of North Carolina at Chapel Hill found that the rate of death from prostate cancer in the United States was significantly lower in the sunbaked South than in the North. The only explanation they had was that people in the South get more UV light, or ultraviolet radiation.

Q: What about other environmental factors?

A: A recent study found that farmers exposed to herbicides were more than twice as likely to develop prostate cancer as farmers who used no herbicides. The study, of 145,000 farmers in Canada, is the first major research connection between herbicides and prostate cancer. However, since the researchers relied on census data, it could well be that other factors, such as diet, led to the different rates of prostate cancer.

As for other occupational exposures, studies show that men who do welding or electroplating, or who make batteries, and are thus exposed to the metal cadmium, may have a higher risk of getting prostate cancer. Workers in the rubber industry also seem to be a risk group.

Q: Have lifestyle factors, like promiscuity, been associated with prostate cancer?

A: There's been speculation that untreated venereal disease or cigarette smoking may also increase risk. But no factor has been linked to prostate cancer the way diet has.

Q: Does it help if I exercise regularly?

A: Absolutely. Data from nearly 18,000 men in the Harvard Alumni Health Study over a 15-year period strongly suggest that a consistent exercise regimen over many years may lessen the risk of developing prostate cancer. While 419 men developed prostate cancer, only one case was found among men who described themselves as highly active in 1962 or 1966, and again in 1977.

Q: Why does exercise seem to help?

A: It's not clear, but one possible explanation is that increased physical activity may lower the level of testosterone, a primary suspect for prostate cancer.

Of course, exercise can also help you control your weight, and that may be a factor in prostate-cancer mortality. The Adventist study showed that obese men were 2½ times more likely to have fatal prostate cancer than men closer to their desirable weight.

Q: Are there any drugs that can prevent prostate cancer?

A: It's purely hypothetical at this point. There are indications that dihydrotestosterone (DHT), which we described in the previous section on BPH, could also be a culprit in promoting prostate cancer. A new drug, finasteride (manufactured by Merck under the brand name Proscar), lowers DHT levels, and the National Cancer Institute is running a prostate-cancer prevention trial to evaluate its effect on men at high risk for prostate cancer.

Proscar must be prescribed by a physician and is now used to treat BPH. Read on in the next chapter for a discussion of that drug and more.

3 TREATMENT FOR BPH

Q: Okay, let's get down to practicalities. The doctor tells me I have BPH. What do I do?

A: Maybe nothing, maybe a whole lot. An enlarged prostate alone is not enough reason to undergo treatment. It's generally agreed in the medical community that BPH requires treatment only if either of two conditions apply: The symptoms are severe enough to be bothersome (for example, you continually feel the urge to urinate and you're retaining large amounts of urine) or the function of the urinary tract is seriously affected.

However, perhaps your symptoms are only moderate—you need to urinate a couple of times during the night, and your flow is weaker—and tests indicate that your bladder and kidneys aren't in any immediate danger. In that case, you may opt for what the medical profession calls "watchful waiting"—that is, you do nothing more than have regular checkups to make sure that the condition isn't worsening and that you're not developing complications from BPH.

Q: Won't the condition inevitably get worse?

A: Not necessarily. In a 1992 issue of *American Health* magazine, Aaron Kirkemo, M.D., a urologist at Henry Ford Hospital in Detroit, noted that "a significant number of men with symptoms will not need surgery. Prostate symptoms fluctuate over time; some get worse, but some get better with no treatment at all."

Q: But what if the condition is uncomfortable or dangerous?

A: Then you've got an almost bewildering number of possibilities: surgical procedures, less invasive procedures like **balloon urethroplasty** and a fairly recent but important addition, medications. The field is changing rapidly, and so are your options. What you choose to do depends on your objectives, age, general health, symptoms and, of course, your economic condition.

Q: You didn't mention my doctor's advice. Shouldn't I follow that?

A: Certainly you should get his opinion, as well as a second and maybe a third. You'll find there's a lot of honest confusion and disagreement among physicians about when and how to treat BPH. This is borne out by a study several years ago by John Wennberg, M.D., of the Dartmouth Medical School. It found that, from one community to another, the probability that an older man would undergo surgery for BPH varied by more than threefold.

In an effort to promote understanding and consistency in the diagnosis and treatment of BPH, the Agency for Health Care Policy and Research, an arm of the U.S. Department of Health and Human Services, has collaborated with the American Urological Association to develop guidelines for both doctors and the public. You can write for a copy at the address listed at the end of this book. Be sure to mark the envelope ''BPH.''

SURGERY

Q: To cut to the core of the matter, then: What's the surgical procedure for BPH?

A: It's called a prostatectomy—really a partial prostatectomy. All of the new tissue that is the result of BPH is removed from the prostatic capsule; the original prostatic tissue is left intact. The prostatic urethra is also removed, but is eventually replaced by normal growth of a new lining that comes down from the bladder.

Q: Is there more than one type of prostatectomy?

A: There are basically two surgical approaches to BPH: open and closed. An open prostatectomy, the method used historically, requires an abdominal incision. Increasingly, the approach used by surgeons is the closed operation, which (unlike the open version) is done without an incision.

There are two kinds of closed operations: **transurethral resection of the prostate (TURP)** and **transurethral incision of the prostate (TUIP)**. About 95 percent of all operations for BPH are TURPs, which some urologists call ''the gold standard'' in BPH treatment, and others describe, more flippantly, as the ''Roto-Rooter'' of prostatectomies.

Let's start with the most commonly performed procedure: the TURP.

Q: What happens in a TURP?

A: In a TURP, the surgeon tunnels through the penis and urethra with a **resectoscope** to resect, or cut, the innermost core of the prostate. The resectoscope, a thin tube about 12 inches in length, contains a light, valves for controlling fluid to irrigate the surgical field, and an electric cutting current or tubular knife blade to cut away tissue. It also has a coagulating electrical current to seal the blood vessels that bleed during the operation.

Starting at the center of the prostatic urethra and working outward, the surgeon removes the obstructing tissue a piece at a time. The pieces of prostate tissue, known as prostate ''chips,'' that have been cut away are carried by the fluid into the bladder, and then flushed out through the resectoscope.

Q: You said earlier that there's a second closed surgical approach to BPH, the TUIP. What is it?

A: A TUIP, or transurethral incision of the prostate, is a more limited surgical procedure than a TURP. Unlike a TURP, a TUIP does not cut away at and flush out the enlarged prostatic tissue. Instead, the surgeon, having tunneled through the urethra, uses the resectoscope to make two deep incisions from a point just inside the bladder neck all the way through the prostate. This has the effect of widening the urinary passage.

Q: What are the other surgical treatments for BPH?

A: There are three open kinds of prostatectomies: the **suprapubic**, the **retropubic**, and the perineal.

The "pubic" refers to the pubic bone and, as the names suggest, each of these involves a different anatomical approach to the enlarged prostate.

Q: What's involved in the suprapubic approach?

A: The surgeon cuts from the navel to the pubic bone, and then into the lower abdomen and bladder in order to reach down into the prostatic urethra. There are two types of suprapubic operations: a "blind" approach, in which the prostate remains concealed, and a visual approach, in which the surgeon makes an incision that allows him to see the bladder neck.

In either case, the surgeon uses his index finger to scoop out the BPH tissue. It's possible to do this by touch, since the BPH tissue yields easily, while the true prostate is more resistant.

Q: What about the retropubic approach?

A: The surgeon makes the same up-and-down incision used in the suprapubic approach, but instead of opening the bladder he cleans the area under the pubic bone and exposes the entire surface of the prostate. Then he makes an incision in the prostate and, again using his finger and curved scissors, cleans out the BPH tissue.

Q: And what does the perineal approach involve?

A: An incision is made through the perineum, between the anus and scrotum, and the prostate is approached from below.

Q: Which of the three open approaches is best?

A: They all have their drawbacks. In a "blind" supra-pubic approach, controlling bleeding after the obstructing prostate tissue has been removed can be a problem; the surgeon can't see the site in order to identify which blood vessels need to be sealed. Recovering from both suprapubic approaches can be quite difficult, because the bladder has been cut and the patient may require two catheters in the bladder for several days to drain the blood and urine.

In the retropubic approach, the exposure of the prostate and bladder neck makes it easy to control bleeding, and recovery is easier. But it can be very hard to expose the prostate in men who are obese or have a narrow or deep bony pelvis.

The perineal approach, which is the oldest of the surgeries for BPH, has a higher risk of causing impotence because the nerves that control erections are exposed during the procedure. For that reason, it's rarely used today.

Q: If I'm having surgery for BPH, should I have a TURP, a TUIP or an open prostatectomy?

A: A number of factors should go into that decision, starting with your physical condition. In general, men who are older or in poorer health are advised to have TURPs because the procedure is physically less demanding. In particular, men who have prostate cancer as well as BPH should avoid open surgery.

Q: Why is that?

A: When cancer has spread from the true prostate, where it began, into BPH tissue, it's often impossible to separate the two tissues during an open prostatectomy. Attempts to remove the BPH tissue may result in tearing the prostate gland right through its true capsule.

Q: What about the recovery period for the different approaches?

A: Anything that involves a lot of cutting is likely to involve more postoperative pain and a longer hospital stay than a procedure requiring a small incision or none at all. After a 90-minute TURP under a spinal anesthetic, you're probably going to be walking around within 24 hours and released from the hospital within a few days. With open surgery, you could be hospitalized for as long as 10 days.

Q: You haven't given any reasons for having open surgery. Are there any?

A: Yes, some very important ones.
    First, most doctors feel that a TURP shouldn't be tried if the prostate is very large: 50 grams or more—more than twice the normal size. However, only about 10 percent of all patients develop a prostate that large.
    Second, open surgery also makes sense for men who need additional procedures performed at the same time, typically bladder repairs like removal of large stones or of diverticula—problems we mentioned in the previous chapter.
    Third, some men have hip problems that make it hard to assume the position required for TURP, which is the

standard position for childbirth: flat on your back, with legs spread and elevated.

Q: So purely physical factors would affect my decision?

A: No, that's not all. A TURP is a somewhat trickier procedure than the open approaches. Prominent urologists agree that if you're not in skilled surgical hands, even if you don't have any of the physical problems cited above, you might want to consider an open prostatectomy. In a later section, we discuss complications of both kinds of approaches.

Q: What about TURP versus TUIP? How do they compare?

A: It's really impossible to say, because TUIP is so little used that there are virtually no data to go on. Urologists who like TUIP say it's most appropriate when the enlargement is fairly small. It's also been reported that TUIP has fewer complications, a subject we address below. However, in *The Prostate Book,* Stephen N. Rous says that, because a TUIP leaves the obstructing tissue behind, it may be less effective than a TURP.

Q: So a TURP is effective?

A: We'd have to give you a "yes, but..." response. It depends a lot on how bad the condition was in the man who was treated.

In general, studies show that men who have acute urinary retention or severe obstruction before surgery receive the greatest benefit from TURPs. For example, a study of 388 men in the south of England who'd undergone TURP during 1988 found the greatest improvement by far was among men whose problems had been the most severe.

Symptoms that the researchers defined as "obstructive," such as hesitancy and fullness, improved more than "irritative" symptoms like frequency and nocturia. The study reports, however, that more than 70 percent of all the men who underwent the procedure said their symptoms overall had decreased and they felt better.

Q: **Why do some men respond better to a TURP than others?**

A: Partly because some men are bothered more by BPH than others. As a study of men in Maine in the 1980s found, men with similar BPH symptoms reported considerable differences in how much they were bothered by those symptoms.

Unlike a lot of medical conditions, BPH is a condition to which men have a highly subjective response. And, despite such tests as urodynamic studies, it's difficult to quantify. Often there's a big difference between the symptoms reported by the men themselves and the clinical evidence, such as the data from urodynamic studies, reported by their doctors.

It's interesting to note that, in clinical trials of various treatments for BPH, researchers report a strong placebo effect: People who received nothing more than the placebo, an inactive substance used as a control in an experiment, often reported a significant improvement in symptoms.

Q: So TURPs are somewhat effective, sometimes. What about open prostatectomies?

A: One widely publicized study indicates that open prostatectomies may be more effective in the long run. Patients in Denmark, England and Canada were studied by Noralou Roos, Ph.D., a researcher at the University of Manitoba, in Canada. She found that, eight years after surgery, the proportion of men undergoing their second prostatectomy (open or closed) was substantially higher after a TURP than after an open prostatectomy. The study, which was published in the *New England Journal of Medicine,* reports that second prostatectomies were between three and six times more common after TURPs.

Q: What do you mean? That BPH comes back?

A: That's right. A prostatectomy, whether open or closed, typically offers only temporary relief from BPH. The reason? The surgery leaves intact the prostate, which is perfectly capable of enlarging a second time.

It's commonly said that the benefit of the operation lasts between 15 and 20 years. Since the typical prostatectomy patient is over 65, most men don't live long enough to require a second procedure. Another way of putting the odds is that 10 percent of the men who have the procedure once will ultimately need it again.

Q: Who's most likely to need a second prostatectomy?

A: Usually the repeater is a man who had the first surgery at an early age. To illustrate that, here's a good example from the front pages of newspapers nationwide. Former President Reagan had his first TURP in 1967, when he was a comparatively young man for the procedure. At the time, he was warned he'd probably need to be TURPed again, and right on schedule, 20 years later and 76 years old, he was back in the operating room.

Q: But didn't you just say that some men were undergoing second prostatectomies within eight years of their first?

A: That's what the Roos study found. And other studies suggest that the 15-to-20-year figure may be on the rosy side. A study led by John Wennberg analyzed the Medicare records of 15,000 men in New England who had had TURPs. It found that about 20 percent of the men had repeat TURPs within five years, presumably because their symptoms had recurred.

Q: Why should the reoperation rate be higher for TURP than for open surgery?

A: Nobody knows. One theory, offered by Stephen Rous, is that the foreign physicians in the study weren't as expert at the operation as those in the United States—hence the higher rate of second TURPs, as well as the greater number of other complications. Without further research, it's hard to know whether the surgeons' skill levels were a critical factor.

Q: With all that repeat surgery, how common are prostatectomies?

A: It's the most common form of major surgery in men over 55 years of age. Several years ago, it was estimated that a 40-year-old man in the United States who lives to the age of 80 would have a 29 percent chance of having a prostatectomy for BPH. The figure has probably increased since then.

Q: Is all that surgery really necessary?

A: A number of studies indicate that some of the operations could be deferred for years, if not indefinitely, as long as the men can live with the symptoms and prefer them to the surgery to ameliorate those symptoms.

A study begun in the 1970s tracked 108 patients who had been advised to have prostate surgery and had refused. Ten years later, 18 of them had finally had surgery to deal with worsening problems, but the other 90, although bothered by their conditions, were still holding out. The 18 who were operated on hadn't been hurt by the delay. Those findings, the researchers conclude, indicate that much surgery could be postponed, perhaps indefinitely.

But, as we said earlier, it all depends on the severity of the symptoms and the men's willingness to tolerate discomfort. An ongoing study of the results of TURP versus watchful waiting for 550 men in nine Veterans Administration hospitals is finding TURP to be "highly effective" when men with mild symptoms are excluded, according to John H. Wasson, M.D., an internist specializing in geriatric medicine at Dartmouth Medical School.

Q: So I should be sure the symptoms are really severe?

A: Yes, and that they're from BPH. As we said in Chapter 2, many people have urinary problems, and there are indications that many of the men who are operated on for BPH don't actually have the condition. In a 1992 article in the *Journal of Urology,* Edward McGuire,

M.D., a urologist at the University of Texas Health Science Center in Houston, said that "we misidentify some 25 to 50 percent of the patients who undergo transurethral resection of the prostate as suffering from obstructive uropathy when, in fact, they do not."

Q: What's the cost of a TURP?

A: The going rate is between $6,000 and $8,000 for the surgery and three years of follow-up. Americans spend at least $3 billion annually for surgery for BPH. Because it's a procedure that's performed most often on older men, Medicare pays for most TURPs in the United States.

Mortality Rates in Surgery

Q: Is prostatectomy a safe procedure?

A: Both open and closed prostatectomies have traditionally been considered very safe procedures, resulting in very few deaths or complications. Various studies report a mortality rate hovering around 1 percent in the first month after either type of procedure—lower for men in their 60s, higher for men in their 80s.

However, a higher mortality rate was reported by Wennberg, Roos and other researchers who analyzed claims data for some 4,600 men over the age of 65 who'd had prostatectomies in Manitoba or Maine in the mid-1970s. Three months after the procedure, whether a TURP or an open prostatectomy, the death rate was higher than expected.

Q: Did the researchers explain why death rates were high?

A: The main factor seemed to be where the surgery took place. Men who'd had either procedure at smaller hospitals (fewer than 150 beds) were 1.8 times more likely to die in the next three months than men who went to hospitals with 300 beds or more, according to the researchers, whose findings were published in the *Journal of the American Medical Association*.

"The magnitude of the death rate following prostatectomy and its variation by hospital suggest the operation should not be viewed as low-risk or 'minor' surgery," the authors conclude. In other words, the quality of the health-care providers and hospitals was critical.

Q: So a TURP and an open prostatectomy have about the same risk?

A: That was that study's implication. But other work by the same researchers suggests that a TURP might actually be riskier.

The Roos study we mentioned earlier, which found a higher rate of second prostatectomies after TURPs, also indicates that TURPs may be less safe than open prostatectomies. The study reports that men undergoing TURPs had a higher mortality rate during the following five years than those who'd received open prostatectomies.

Even after "risk-adjusting" the data to reflect the fact that open-prostatectomy patients tend to be healthier, the researchers found that men who'd undergone a TURP were 1½ times more likely to die within five years than those who'd had open surgery.

Q: Does that mean that open surgery is actually safer than a TURP?

A: As you can imagine, the findings were hotly disputed. The *New England Journal of Medicine,* which published the study, editorialized that it "does not provide convincing evidence that open prostatectomy carries less risk than TURP."

A few years later, urologists breathed a sigh of relief when John Concato, M.D., at the Yale University School of Medicine reported, in a study published in the *New England Journal of Medicine* in 1992, that TURPs and open prostatectomies had similar mortality rates five years after the procedure. The reason for any seeming difference, Concato said, was that older, sicker patients underwent TURPs.

Q: So what's the bottom line: Is TURP as safe as open surgery, or not?

A: It's still a controversial issue in urological circles, and researchers agree that more study is desirable. However, because TURP has virtually supplanted every other surgical approach, it's getting harder to analyze the relative merits of TURP over other procedures.

Q: If the Roos findings are accurate, why would TURP have a higher mortality rate than open surgery?

A: Roos stated that the "most striking difference in the risk of death"—a relative risk of 2.5 in TURP patients—came from heart attacks. But it's not at all clear why a TURP would lead to a heart attack. British researchers, noting that cardiac output, which is the amount of blood pumped by the heart, falls after a TURP, suggest that the absorption of irrigation fluid that is used to keep the surgical area clear of blood during the procedure may somehow affect the heart and lead to a heart attack. Still, that's only a guess.

Complications of Surgery

Q: **Okay, what are the documented complications of prostatectomies?**

A: You've probably heard that surgery for BPH leads to **impotence**, or loss of erection, and **incontinence**, or loss of urinary control. It's true that all of the surgical approaches to BPH, including TURP, involve some risks in those areas, but they're not nearly as bad as you may think.

Q: **What precisely are the odds of each condition developing?**

A: Short-term incontinence is fairly common, but only a small percentage of the men who have prostatectomies continue to have problems over the long run. As for impotence, it can take up to a year to recover sexual function, but ultimately most men who are able to have erections before the procedure recover that ability.

It's difficult to give precise numbers because, particularly in the case of sexual function, many men had problems well before they underwent surgery. Obviously surgery isn't the only cause of either impotence or incontinence. As we say in Chapter 2, the bladder muscle itself may have been permanently weakened by the extra work it had to do when the prostate became so enlarged that it obstructed urine flow.

Q: Why would a prostatectomy cause incontinence?

A: You control urine flow through two mechanisms: the muscles that surround the prostate gland and maintain the tone of the prostatic urethra and bladder neck; and the external urethral sphincter. It's possible for either mechanism to get damaged during a TURP.

Even if the external, or voluntary, sphincter isn't damaged by the operation, it may already have become weakened from disuse. That's because, for months or probably years before the operation, the prostate itself became the main shutoff valve when you urinated. When the external sphincter is damaged, you may have a condition known as **stress incontinence**.

Q: What's stress incontinence?

A: In stress incontinence, you may involuntarily leak urine when increased pressure within your abdomen squeezes down on your bladder. Such pressure can occur when you sneeze, cough, laugh or exert yourself physically by, say, lifting a heavy weight. It's found most often in women who have given birth vaginally, but it can also affect men after prostate surgery.

Q: Are there degrees of incontinence? How bad is mine likely to be?

A: That depends on how much damage is done to either of the mechanisms we described. If the musculature around the prostate is damaged, you can become completely incontinent. However, that's extremely rare after BPH surgery. Stress incontinence, which involves minor losses of urine, is more likely.

Q: Can incontinence and impotence be treated?

A: Because impotence occurs far more often as a side effect of therapy for prostate cancer, we discuss the condition and various treatments in Chapter 4.

Incontinence can be lessened or cured, depending upon how far you want to go with various treatments. There's a wide range of options, including surgical remedies, medication, continuous catheterization and external collection devices called condom catheters. Even something as simple as weight loss, if you're obese, may ease your symptoms. There are also many treatments that you can do yourself as soon as your catheter is removed.

Below, we discuss several therapies. For more information, at the back of this book we've listed some groups that specialize in helping people who are incontinent.

Q: What are some of the self-help techniques?

A: Pelvic muscle exercises are at the top of the list. Although they've been recommended primarily for women after childbirth, they appear to help men, too, particularly if the men have mild stress incontinence.

To do these exercises, you must first identify the specific muscles that are responsible for closing the urethra and stopping the flow of urine. If you don't know which ones they are, try tightening your muscles while you're actually urinating. You should practice contracting these muscles repeatedly, for 10 seconds each time, over a period of weeks or months. Just how frequently you need to do the exercises to rebuild muscle strength is disputed; some recommend "periodic" exercise, while others call for 1,000 contractions a day. You should discuss an exercise regimen with your doctor.

Q: Are there other self-help methods that work well?

A: Biofeedback is one that's widely used. It employs electrical monitoring devices, inserted into the rectum, that monitor your movements and give you minute-to-minute information on how well you're controlling your sphincter. One biofeedback study at the University of Pittsburgh, of men who were incontinent after prostate surgery, reported an 80 percent reduction in leakage.

While biofeedback is characterized as self-help, it requires a little outside help from professionals, and that costs time and effort. You'll need to find a therapist who's trained in the technique, and you'll probably need to go to a clinic at least once a week for a few months. You'll need to use the device at home, too. Your insurance company can tell you whether it covers such treatments.

Q: What can I do about incontinence if self-help isn't enough?

A: At the other end of the spectrum is a comparatively elaborate device called an **artificial urinary sphincter**. It's a **prosthesis** consisting of a balloon that fills with urine, a cuff that encircles the urethra, and a pump implanted in your scrotum—all of which are connected by tubing. To urinate, you squeeze the pump in your scrotum. The device, which prevents involuntary leakage, is generally recommended for people who suffer from severe incontinence.

Q: What are the pros and cons?

A: According to Rebecca Chalker and Kristene E. Whitmore, authors of *Overcoming Bladder Disorders,* doctors who have implanted the device report that between 75 and 85 percent of their patients are satisfied with it. In 10 to 15 percent of the men who have an artificial sphincter, the authors say, "mechanical failures and tissue degeneration in the area of the implants have occurred. Like most mechanical devices, an artificial sphincter may break or wear out after a while and may need to be replaced; so before you decide to get a sphincter implanted, you should be aware that you may need a second surgery to remove or replace it."

Q: I've heard that, even if a prostatectomy doesn't cause impotence, it produces something called a "dry orgasm." What's that?

A: Most men do develop a condition called dry orgasm, or **retrograde ejaculation**, after prostatectomy. To explain what it is, first we'd better describe what happens during a normal orgasm.

During sexual activity, sperm from the testicles enter the urethra near the opening of the bladder. Normally, a muscle blocks off the entrance to the bladder, the external sphincter opens, and contracting muscles of the urethra expel the sperm-laden semen through the penis.

During a prostatectomy, however, the bladder neck is frequently enlarged and thus cannot close completely. So when the muscles of the urethra contract, the semen is ejaculated backward through the open internal sphincter and into the bladder. Later the semen gets flushed out in the urine.

Q: Is that serious?

A: If you can't ejaculate semen, you can't reproduce— or at least, not in the tried-and-true way. Fortunately, most men who undergo prostatectomies already have their families and are well past the age when they want more. As for the sensation of dry orgasm, many men say it feels peculiar but not unpleasant. It simply takes getting used to. However, if you believe that retrograde ejaculation could be a serious problem for you, some urologists say you should consider an alternative procedure, such as TUIP, that is less likely to result in this condition.

Q: But what if I do still want children? Can anything be done?

A: Yes, you can try **artificial insemination**, a method widely used in cases of infertility. In a doctor's office, your sperm would be extracted from your urine after retrograde ejaculation. It would then be deposited in your partner's vagina.

Q: Are there any other complications from prostatectomies?

A: Yes. Another common complication is urethral stricture, or scarring, which decreases the size of the channel through which urine flows and creates an obstruction as bad as or worse than the problem that led to a TURP in the first place. This generally happens if the resectoscope used in a TURP is too large for the urethra.

According to Stephen Rous, between 10 and 15 percent of the men who have TURPs develop strictures. Usually a doctor can resolve the problem by stretching the urethra, during an office visit.

In a very few cases, the bladder neck gets cut instead of BPH tissue. When it heals, it scars and shrinks so badly that there's only a pinhole opening for urine. When this happens, the patient may need a repeat operation, similar to a TUIP, to widen the bladder neck.

Q: Are bacterial infections common?

A: They're not common, but they do happen. Some doctors prescribe preventive antibiotics for several weeks following prostate surgery; others wait to see if infection actually occurs.

One possible complication is **epididymitis**, an inflammation and enlargement of the epididymis, the sperm-carrying structure we mention in Chapter 1. It can result from infected urine. You also run a slight risk of developing a persistent bacterial infection after prostate surgery from conditions such as incomplete bladder emptying (which may be due to incomplete removal of obstructing BPH tissue) and obstruction of a kidney that has bacteria in it.

ALTERNATIVE PROCEDURES

Q: You mentioned balloon urethroplasty as a less invasive procedure. What's involved?

A: Balloon urethroplasty, or **balloon dilatation** of the urethra, works on the same principle as balloon treatment for coronary arteries. The tissue causing the obstruction isn't removed, just pushed out of the way.

In balloon urethroplasty, a doctor inserts a thin tube with a balloon on its tip into the opening of the penis.

She guides it to the narrowed portion of the urethra,
where the balloon is inflated. This action compresses the
prostate and widens the urethra, easing the flow of urine.
The 15-minute procedure can be done in a urologist's
office under local anesthesia.

Q: Does it eliminate BPH?

A: The procedure is still relatively new, so there's
little long-term data. So far, most of the evidence
points to temporary relief. But that's all it is: temporary.
While men who've had the procedure report that it
became much easier initially to urinate, indications are
that the symptoms of BPH return fairly soon.

One study found that balloon dilatation and cystoscopy
—a diagnostic procedure that isn't designed to relieve
symptoms—had about the same effect. Studies at the Mayo
Clinic indicate that the effect of balloon urethroplasty
may not last beyond a year or two, and only for a limited
group of men.

Q: Like who?

A: Doctors who've worked with the treatment say
the best candidates are younger men who have
relatively mild symptoms—prostates that aren't terribly
enlarged, urinary retention that's not too bad—and who
express considerable concern about their ability to
maintain erections and to ejaculate.

Balloon urethroplasty could also provide welcome
relief for people who are high surgical risks, such as men
with advanced prostate cancer and urinary retention, and
nursing-home patients who require catheters.

Q: What are the alternatives to the balloon?

A: There's growing interest in **hyperthermia**, a procedure first used with good results to treat obstructions in men with prostate cancer. Also known as **thermotherapy**, hyperthermia involves the application of heat to the enlarged prostate. There are two approaches, through either the rectum or the urethra, but both combine microwave heating with conductive cooling.

Q: What's the difference between the two approaches to heat therapy?

A: In **transurethral hyperthermia**, a modified Foley catheter containing a microwave antenna is inserted through the urethra and heats the tissues deep within the prostate to 45 °C (113 °F) or higher. Cold water runs through the catheter, to provide some comfort and prevent heating up (and possibly shrinking or killing) tissue in the prostatic urethra. The procedure, which takes about an hour, can be carried out in a urologist's office with only local anesthesia.

In **transrectal hyperthermia**, the water-cooled catheter is placed in the rectum, and the temperature of the prostate tissue is heated to about 43 °C (109 °F). This one-hour treatment requires no anesthesia, but it involves several more applications than the transurethral approach. It's administered two times weekly over the course of a month or two.

Q: How does the heat work?

A: Strangely enough, nobody really knows. When the transrectal approach is used, the prostate shrinks very little and there's no sign of the **necrosis**, or tissue death, that would reduce the enlarged gland. It's been suggested that the heat relaxes muscle tissue in the prostate, easing the tightening around the urethra.

With transurethral heat therapy, there's definite necrosis of the enlarged prostate, and the obstruction shrinks.

Q: But heat therapy is believed to be effective?

A: Yes, and the more heat, the more effective. In various studies, both approaches got excellent marks; most of the men who were treated said their urinary problems improved significantly, and urodynamic studies tended to confirm the men's subjective reports.

The procedure is still relatively new and untested, however, and we don't have much indication of its long-term efficacy. In one study, about one-third of the men given transrectal hyperthermia required surgery for BPH sometime within the next four years. On the other hand, two-thirds of the men didn't need surgery.

Q: Are there any complications with heat therapy, or cases in which it shouldn't be used?

A: Men with greatly enlarged prostates may be poor candidates for hyperthermia, as their glands are hard to reach. For all men, the middle lobe of the prostate is also hard to reach, and that, unfortunately, is usually responsible for the obstruction.

As for complications, occasionally the transrectal approach has resulted temporarily in painful urination or bloody urine. But no major complications, such as impotence or retrograde ejaculation, have been reported so far.

Q: If it's so good, why isn't heat therapy more widely used?

A: It is being used extensively in Israel and Europe, but it hasn't yet received a go-ahead from our own Food and Drug Administration. The technique has been undergoing clinical trials at a few centers in the United States since early 1991, however. A number of questions still need to be answered, such as optimum temperature, best route, how long each treatment should last, and who should receive them.

Another problem with heat therapy is that the Prostathermers or Prostatrons, as the machines are called by their manufacturers, are quite elaborate, with computer consoles, treatment modules and ultrasound machines—and price tags to match. As of this writing, the cost is about $1 million. In the long run, however, since the procedure is about one-third the price of a TURP, the machine could pay for itself.

Q: Are any other nonsurgical procedures being developed?

A: Urologists in Europe are investigating the use of springlike coiled devices and stainless-steel **stents**, which are inserted into the prostatic urethra to stretch it and let urine flow more easily. Both devices, which may remain in place indefinitely, have been tolerated fairly well, and patients have reported relief from urinary problems. But because the devices are so new, it's too soon to say whether they provide more than short-term relief.

A still more experimental procedure is **ultrasonic aspiration** of the prostate. Using a device similar to a resectoscope, inserted through the urethra, a doctor directs ultrasound vibrations against the enlarged portion of the prostate and "disrupts" the BPH tissue, which is then aspirated, or sucked out, through the urethra.

There's also been an effort to apply **cryosurgery** to BPH. In this treatment, probes are inserted into the prostate through the urethra, and liquid nitrogen is circulated through the probes to freeze and kill the BPH tissue. The tissue is then flushed out through a catheter. While the procedure seems to work, a number of men who've been treated have developed infections and hemorrhaging. Cryosurgery may be better at treating prostate cancer than BPH, as we discuss in the next chapter.

Q: I thought lasers were the cutting edge in medicine. Doesn't anybody use lasers to get rid of BPH?

A: Scientists are investigating the use of **transurethral ultrasound-guided laser-induced prostatectomy**—a procedure with the happy acronym of TULIP—as an alternative to surgery, but it's still highly experimental.

This is how it works: A laser probe is inserted into the urethra. Using an ultrasound probe in the rectum to direct the laser energy, the doctor uses the beam to superheat and destroy BPH tissue. A week or two later, the dead tissue sloughs out. A variation known as visual laser ablation of the prostate uses a microtelescope to guide the laser into position.

MEDICATION

Q: So much for cutting and probing—are there drugs that can treat BPH?

A: There's been a lot of talk lately about the "prostate pill." It's clearly an idea whose time has come, but the pill itself has yet to be developed. That's the bad news. The good news is that, after all these years, there are drugs in the pipeline that may eventually offer a real alternative to surgery.

Q: What are the drugs?

A: There are two major categories. The first is **anti-hypertensives**, which have the effect of relaxing the smooth muscle tissue in the prostate and bladder neck, easing constriction of the urethra. These are also known as **alpha-adrenergic blockers**.

The second category is 5-alpha-reductase inhibitors. They inhibit the production of DHT, which, as we discuss in Chapter 2, seems to be responsible for prostate enlargement.

Scientists are also investigating a third drug category: **aromatase** inhibitors. The enzyme aromatase converts testosterone into the form of estrogen that is found in all men. It may contribute to BPH in older men who, as part of the normal aging process, develop higher amounts of estrogen relative to testosterone. Aromatase drugs, such as atamestane, block this action. Research in this category, however, is in the early stages.

Q: Back up a bit! Aren't antihypertensives for people with high blood pressure?

A: That's right. In fact, their potential for treating BPH was first noticed when it was reported in 1978 that one of the drugs, prazosin (brand name Minipress, manufactured by Pfizer), resulted in urinary incontinence in women who were being treated for hypertension. Since then, more than a dozen clinical trials have been run on prazosin, terazosin (brand name Hytrin, manufactured by Abbott), doxazosin (brand name Cardura, manufactured by Pfizer) and other drugs, exploring their use in the treatment of BPH.

Q: What do the drug tests show?

A: While most of the clinical trials have been too limited and brief to produce definitive results, early returns are encouraging. In a series of studies by the National Center for Treatment and Research of Prostate Diseases, in Milwaukee, terazosin was found to improve patients' urinary flow rates considerably, although there was less progress in eliminating irritative symptoms, such as nocturia.

Q: Are there side effects?

A: Antihypertensive drugs have a well-established list of adverse reactions and side effects, and obviously there's some trepidation about their regular use by people whose blood pressure is normal.

The Milwaukee studies and others have reported many side effects in a small number of men taking the drugs we've named. They include headaches, dizziness, flulike symptoms, fatigue, diarrhea, a dramatic drop in blood pressure on standing or sitting up suddenly, nasal stuffiness, fluid retention and heart palpitations.

Q: That doesn't sound so good. Is there any way to minimize side effects?

A: Some doctors tell their patients to take antihypertensives at bedtime or after a substantial meal. Many of the side effects subside after a few days or weeks of drug therapy.

Q: Are any of the antihypertensive drugs you've mentioned already on the market?

A: Yes, although in the United States they're officially approved only for treating hypertension. That situation may change soon. A few months before this book went to press, an advisory committee of the Food and Drug Administration recommended approval of Hytrin for treating BPH. Now the entire FDA has to review the panel's recommendation.

Things are farther along in other countries. Prazosin, for example, is already approved for the treatment of BPH in a number of countries in Europe, as well as in Japan and Australia.

Q: So I can't take these drugs for BPH?

A: On the contrary. Since they're already on the market, many of the drugs are being prescribed specifically for enlarged prostates. The FDA says that about 20 percent of all Hytrin prescriptions, for instance, are written for BPH. Some of these drugs are also being prescribed for other conditions that involve the function of the urethral sphincter muscle, including prostatodynia, when other treatments have failed.

Q: Isn't there any drug approved specifically to treat BPH?

A: Yes. It's finasteride, better known as Proscar, the name under which it's being marketed by Merck & Co. The FDA approved Proscar in mid-1992 and, as of this writing, it's the only drug specifically approved to treat BPH. However, SmithKline Beecham is running clinical trials on a rival product.

Finasteride is in the second category of drugs we mentioned earlier: It belongs to a new family of agents called 5 alpha-reductase inhibitors, which work by blocking the conversion of testosterone into DHT. We mention the 5 alpha-reductase enzyme in the section on BPH in Chapter 2.

Q: Is Proscar effective against BPH?

A: So-so. It seems to be especially effective in shrinking enlarged prostates and keeping them shrunk. But many urologists note that it's less effective at symptom relief. In 12-month clinical trials, Merck found that urine flow increased and other symptoms improved in less than half of the men taking the drug.

"For patients with advanced disease, surgery remains the treatment of choice," says Reginald Bruskewitz, M.D., of the University of Wisconsin Clinical Science Center. "However, Proscar offers a medical option for many patients."

Q: What about complications? Doesn't Proscar cause impotence?

A: You'd expect that, since it's tampering with DHT levels. Circulating testosterone remains high, however, so there's usually no effect on a man's ability to have erections. In its clinical trials, Merck found that 3.7 percent of the subjects became impotent, 3.3 percent reported decreased libido, and 2.8 percent ejaculated less semen when they had orgasm. Some men also reported a general physical weakness.

Q: What about other side effects?

A: Perhaps of greater concern to the medical community is that finasteride lowers serum concentrations of prostate-specific antigen by up to 50 percent. Since, as we discuss in the previous chapter, the PSA test is being used increasingly to screen for prostate cancer, there's a lot of concern that Proscar can make it difficult to detect cancer.

Merck has said that doctors can easily factor in Proscar's impact on PSA levels when they test for prostate cancer. Urological experts say they don't know whether that's really feasible, however. Nor do they know whether men who develop prostate cancer will have elevated PSA levels if they're taking Proscar.

Q: Does that mean that Proscar increases the risk of prostate cancer?

A: Not at all. In fact, just the opposite may be true. Men with the genetic 5-alpha-reductase deficiency (see Chapter 2) don't often get prostate cancer. As we said earlier, Proscar is a 5-alpha-reductase inhibitor. The National Cancer Institute is conducting studies to determine whether finasteride can be used to prevent prostate cancer.

Q: Basically, though, Proscar is safe?

A: So far, it seems safe for men. But it may be quite dangerous for women!

Q: Why is that?

A: Animal studies have shown that Proscar can harm male fetuses. So, although the drug is present in male semen only in minute amounts, women who are or may become pregnant should avoid being exposed to the semen of men taking Proscar. That means no sexual relations—at least not without the use of condoms.

In addition, women who are or may become pregnant should avoid handling crushed tablets of Proscar, so that they don't absorb the drug through their skin.

Q: What does it cost?

A: Proscar, which is to be taken daily in a 5 milligram dose, costs users about $650 a year. That's a bitter pill to swallow, especially if you've got to take it daily for the rest of your life. Once men stop taking finasteride, serum DHT returns to its previous level within two weeks, and BPH symptoms come back.

You may be able to cut your costs slightly through a program Merck launched with Proscar. All new patients get an initial 30 days free. After six months of therapy with Proscar, you can receive a free 30-day supply. After that, until at least 1995, you can get a free one-month supply for every 12 months on Proscar. Your doctor should have details on this program, if you're interested.

Q: Why is Merck doing that?

A: Proscar has been running into resistance from urologists, who say the drug is less effective than surgery. So the pharmaceutical manufacturer, which stands to make millions of dollars on Proscar, is marketing it more directly to you, the consumer.

Q: It's still awfully expensive. Is it covered by insurance?

A: It depends on your specific health-insurance plan. *American Druggist* reported in 1992 that several large health maintenance organizations (HMOs) had decided not to put Proscar on their list of approved prescription drugs because they'd decided it's not worth the cost.

Of course, you may disagree. It's true that, in the long run, TURP may actually be less expensive than Proscar. But the man who's facing the knife or the resectoscope may have a different point of view.

Q: But what if I want to choose between drugs? Which is better, the muscle relaxant or finasteride?

A: Both have their pros and cons. The muscle relaxants work faster, alleviating symptoms within a few weeks rather than the three to six months required by finasteride. But finasteride has more impressive results in shrinking the prostate and could be used to prevent further prostate growth.

Q: So should I take both drugs?

A: Actually, there's a lot of interest in the medical community in combining the two drugs with atamestane, the aromatase inhibitor we mentioned earlier. Finasteride has its greatest effect on the glandular parts of the prostate, while the muscle relaxants act mainly on the prostate's muscle and connective tissue. So doctors feel there might be potential in a drug combination that relaxes the prostatic muscle while shrinking the prostatic tissue.

"I think eventually there will be combination pills containing finasteride, terazosin and atamestane that treat BPH with three different mechanisms," Joseph E. Oesterling, M.D., a urologist with the Mayo Clinic, told *American Druggist* in 1992.

Q: But they all seem pretty problematic right now?

A: Insiders agree that we're seeing just the first wave of medical therapy for BPH. Merck is already working on a more potent "son of Proscar." There may also be alpha blockers that work more selectively, binding only to the alpha receptors on the prostate and bladder that relax the muscle. This would produce fewer side effects.

Q: What about other hormonal therapies? Aren't there drugs to treat BPH by reducing testosterone?

A: Yes, but you may not want to take them.
Consider the results of a small study at the Johns Hopkins University Medical School. The research looked at **nafarelin acetate**, a hormone blocker that inhibits the production of testosterone. After four months, the subjects' prostates had shrunk by one-fourth, and most of the men reported that their urinary problems had improved.

All nine men in the study became temporarily impotent, however. (A tenth subject withdrew after two months, claiming that the loss of libido and drive had hurt his business performance!)

Six months after the medication was stopped, both the men's prostate size and their testosterone levels had returned to the point they were at before treatment. The researchers concluded that the treatment would be appropriate only for a select group of men who couldn't tolerate surgery.

Q: What about estrogen therapy?

A: Same problem. While it's true that estrogens shrink the prostate enough to relieve symptoms, they also lead to impotence and enlarged, tender breasts.

SELF-HELP

Q: Isn't there anything I can do myself to treat the enlargement or at least alleviate the symptoms?

A: As we discuss in Chapter 2, many people, within and without the medical profession, believe that zinc promotes a healthy prostate. Irving M. Bush, M.D., a urologist at the Chicago Medical School, has put some people on zinc therapy for 20 years and says they seem to need prostate surgery far less often than the norm.

He believes that zinc therapy is effective for BPH if it's begun when the prostate first starts to enlarge. The zinc in the body, in his view, keeps the prostate's glandular tissue from enlarging in order to produce more zinc. Bush offers some patients a combination of zinc and muscle relaxants.

Q: Is there anything besides zinc that seems effective?

A: One homeopathic treatment that's been recommended is a combination of three of the amino acids—glycine, alanine and glutamate—in a daily dosage of several grams. Some people say they've been helped by lecithin, and by calcium and magnesium tablets, both of which are available from pharmacists and health-food shops. Certain medicinal herbs have also been found helpful.

4 TREATMENT OF PROSTATE CANCER

Q: I have prostate cancer. What do I do about it?

A: The main treatment options are surgery (usually a procedure called a radical prostatectomy), **radiation therapy**, **hormonal therapy**, and various combinations of all three. Still other treatments are more experimental.

Clinical trials for new treatments, as well as for different combinations of established therapies, are going on in most parts of the country, for most stages of prostate cancer. If you're interested in participating in such research, talk to your doctor or contact the National Cancer Institute (NCI) at the listing shown at the end of this book. NCI's computerized resource of cancer-treatment information, PDQ, has an up-to-date list of clinical trials in progress all over the country.

In this chapter, we discuss the full range of treatments. But there are some important issues to cover before we get down to specifics.

Q: Are all the treatments supposed to do the same thing—wipe out the cancer?

A: No. Radical prostatectomies and radiation therapy are considered **curative** therapies, meaning that they may be capable of destroying the cancer altogether. Hormonal therapy is **palliative**; it can reduce the symptoms of the disease and slow its growth, but hormone therapy doesn't wipe it out.

If you're weighing different treatments for cancer, there's another term you should learn: **adjuvant**. Adjuvant treatment is any therapy that's offered after the most effective form of therapy has been tried.

Q: What about nontreatment? Is that an option?

A: It's a very important option for many men. Because of their slow growth, some small, early-stage prostate cancers may not require treatment, especially when they're in men who are older or have other serious illnesses. Other cancers may be so far advanced that any treatment other than pain management may even be cruel.

Furthermore, as we discuss later in this chapter, treatment is sometimes no more effective than watchful waiting. In summing up the "to treat or not to treat" dilemma, Willet F. Whitmore Jr., M.D., of Memorial Sloan-Kettering Cancer Center in New York, has asked: "Is cure possible in those for whom it is necessary and is cure necessary in those for whom it is possible?"

Q: How do I know what's best for me?

A: The kind of treatment you receive should depend on the stage of your disease, your age and your overall condition. We discuss all these in this chapter.

You should keep in mind that there's great uncertainty, even within the medical profession, about which treatments are most appropriate for various forms of prostate cancer, especially for stages A and B. In a recent editorial in the *Journal of the American Medical Association*, Whitmore wrote that the "optimal management of clinically localized prostatic cancer may be more a matter of opinion, than a matter of fact."

If you find all this uncertainty disturbing, remember that it's generating a lot of work by researchers to find both causes and treatments, and their findings may ultimately benefit you.

SURGERY

Q: What's a radical prostatectomy?

A: A radical prostatectomy is major surgery in which the entire prostate and the seminal vesicles are removed. It's not to be confused with the very limited prostatectomies for BPH that we describe in the previous chapter, and it's not nearly as common—yet. A recent study found that, due to the increase in the rate of reported prostate cancer and improvements in the procedure, the number of radical prostatectomies for Medicare recipients rose nearly sixfold between 1984 and 1990.

A radical prostatectomy is a complicated operation that takes a few hours. After the prostate is removed, the urinary tract is essentially reconstructed. The bladder is

brought down into the pelvis and the bladder neck is
stitched to the stump of the urethra at the point where
the prostate gland was detached from it. This bridges the
gap where the prostate had been, and reestablishes the
lower urinary tract.

Q: Where's the incision?

A: There are two different approaches to a radical
prostatectomy, similar to two approaches described
in Chapter 3 for partial prostatectomies for BPH. One is
retropubic, approaching the prostate from behind and
under the pubic bone. The other is perineal, approaching
the prostate through the perineum (the space between the
scrotum and the anus).

Q: Which is preferable?

A: Both have their pros and cons. The retropubic
prostatectomy has the advantage of allowing the
surgeon to take out the lymph nodes for study by a
pathologist before he continues—or, if the cancer has
spread, doesn't continue—with the operation. That's not
possible during a perineal prostatectomy, so a prostate-
cancer patient may need two separate procedures, several
days apart: an abdominal incision to check out his lymph
nodes and a perineal incision to remove his prostate.

Q: It sounds like there's no reason to have the perineal approach. Is that right?

A: No, there are drawbacks to the retropubic approach, too. The recovery is harder, because an

abdominal incision is considerably more uncomfortable than a perineal incision. And with the retropubic approach, it's somewhat more difficult to expose and remove the prostate.

Q: Is recovery hard after a radical prostatectomy?

A: There's considerable pain immediately afterward. You'll have bladder spasms and, because your intestine isn't contracting normally at first, you'll have a tube draining your abdomen for a few days. A Foley catheter, which we described earlier, is inserted through your penis and into your bladder for about three weeks after the operation. When the catheter is removed, you may be somewhat incontinent for several weeks or even months.

Q: Who should have a radical prostatectomy?

A: Two conditions traditionally have had to be met. First, the cancer must be encapsulated within the prostate. Men with stages A and B1 cancer are the main candidates for radical prostatectomies, although recently the operation has also been used to treat some patients with stage B2 cancer with large nodules.

If your lymph nodes are found to be cancerous while you're on the table for a radical prostatectomy, you'll probably be stitched up at once and sent on to a recovery room. When you come to, you and your doctor will have to discuss what other treatments, such as hormone therapy, you can try.

But we should note that, increasingly, doctors are proceeding with the prostatectomy anyway. One reason is that the surgery itself has become safer. In addition, there's some indication that a prostatectomy is beneficial even when the cancer has already spread.

Q: Even if the cancer has spread beyond the prostate, why shouldn't the prostate be removed?

A: As we indicated, there's disagreement on that point. The traditional view is that, when the cancer has metastasized, there's nothing to be gained—and a lot of unnecessary suffering to be undergone—from removing the prostate. However, some scientists believe that, since new deposits of cancer can come only from the original site, it may be useful to attack the cancer in the prostate.

Q: Is there any research on the impact of radical prostatectomy when the cancer is advanced?

A: Yes, some very interesting research, by the Mayo Clinic is being done. Researchers there have been evaluating the impact of either radical prostatectomy or radiation on stage D1 patients who have also had their testicles removed. (As we discuss later, that's one kind of hormonal therapy.)

The researchers report a better survival rate for men who undergo combined therapies rather than hormonal therapy alone. At the end of five years, men who'd had both their prostates and testicles removed had a 91 percent survival rate, compared with 66 percent for men who'd had only their testicles removed. At 10 years, the rates were 78 percent and 39 percent, respectively.

Q: What's the second condition for a prostatectomy?

A: There's an unofficial age cutoff for a radical pros-tatectomy. The unofficial consensus among doctors seems to be that a man over the age of 70 shouldn't have the operation because it probably wouldn't give him many, if any, additional years, and might even subtract from what he's got left.

That the medical profession is taking this approach was confirmed by a study, published by the Rand Corporation in 1991, of the care received by some 250 men with prostate cancer stages A2 through D1. The study found that older men received fewer diagnostic evaluations and therapies, regardless of their stage of cancer or the hospital in which they were being treated. Men between 50 and 64 received radical prostatectomies and/or radiation, while the treatment for men over 75 was hormonal therapy.

Q: Why would treatment be determined by a man's age?

A: To put it bluntly: because an older man will probably die of something else—a stroke or heart disease, for example—before prostate cancer does him in. Maybe you don't like the idea that doctors are making actuarial calculations worthy of insurance companies. But the fact is that many would consider it brutal to subject a man to treatment for prostate cancer if the tumor isn't likely to be the cause of his death.

Another reason that's given sometimes is that prostatic cancer is more aggressive in younger men. However, a lot of research now indicates that prostate cancer doesn't grow any faster in young men than it does in senior citizens.

Q: It sounds like age discrimination. Is that fair?

A: As the Rand researcher notes, the pattern of care was undoubtedly dictated partly by the patients themselves and partly by concern over their ability to tolerate therapy. In other cases, the doctors may have

arbitrarily chosen 70 as the cutoff. Whether or not that's fair is a question we'll leave to medical ethicists. But it's worth noting that more people are recognizing two concerns: that treatment may be ineffective and even counterproductive, and that health-care resources are limited.

Q: Does that mean that, if I'm 70, I can't get a prostatectomy?

A: Many urologists bend the rule. They're aware that, although the life expectancy from birth of an American man is around 72, once he reaches that age he can expect to live another 10 years. And more and more men are living to the age of 90 and 100. In *The Prostate Book,* Stephen Rous says that "when a patient is in excellent condition and he is a physiological age 65 even though a chronological 75, I think that exceptions should be made."

In fact, in the study we cited earlier on the increase in radical prostatectomies, 12 percent of the procedures were performed on men age 75 or more.

Q: Is a radical prostatectomy safe?

A: As with any major surgery, there are risks. Studies show that about 1 percent of patients die from the procedure, and that's when it's performed at top-rated hospitals. There's also a slight risk of infection, **fistula** or rectal injury, and a higher risk—between 9 and 18 percent —of bladder stricture, or scarring.

Q: Does the procedure cause impotence?

A: A decade or two ago, virtually all prostatectomies resulted in impotence. Surgeons didn't recognize that a pair of nerve bundles close to the prostate control erections, so they inadvertently stretched or tore the nerves during radical prostatectomies. Then in 1982 Patrick Walsh, M.D., a urologist at the Johns Hopkins University School of Medicine, identified the cobweblike nerves and devised the famous nerve-sparing procedure that allows surgeons to remove the prostate while leaving the nerves intact.

Now, while most men take several months to two years to recover full potency, permanent impotence after nerve-sparing surgery is the exception rather than the rule. In fact, radical prostatectomies, when appropriate, are more likely to be recommended for men who are still potent and healthy than are other treatments, which have a higher rate of impotence.

Q: What are the statistics now for prostatectomies and impotence?

A: Walsh recently analyzed the results of some 600 men who underwent nerve-sparing prostatectomies at Johns Hopkins between 1982 and 1988, and reported that, of the 500 who were potent before surgery, 68 percent were potent at least 18 months after surgery.

The best results were in men under the age of 50 and in men with tumors in an earlier stage. Walsh also found that men could remain potent if only one of the nerve bundles was preserved.

Q: So I've got a 70 percent chance of remaining potent?

A: Yes, under optimal conditions and with a surgeon who's mastered the technique. As Barry E. Epstein, M.D., a radiation oncologist at Fox Chase Cancer Center, in Philadelphia, has noted tactfully, ''There is as yet no evidence that the average urologist performs the anatomic [nerve-sparing] radical prostatectomy with outcomes comparable to those of the few centers of surgical expertise that publish results.'' In other words, if you're considering a nerve-sparing prostatectomy, you better examine your surgeon's track record.

Q: Is there anything I can do if I become impotent?

A: Any man can regain the ability to have rigid erections, depending on his willingness to try mechanical solutions or other methods. There are several kinds of treatments, ranging from penile injections and vacuum devices, to protheses.

Q: Can you describe each treatment?

A: The most widely used remedy for impotence is self-injection, in which the man injects into his penis a couple of drops of a drug that relaxes arterial muscles and allows blood to flow into the penis. The drug may be a synthetic version of a natural hormone called prosta-glandin E-1, alone or in combination with other drugs.

A vacuum device puts negative pressure on the penis, making it bigger and longer. A tight rubber band is applied to the base of the penis, holding the erection in place.

A penile prothesis is a device that, surgically implanted within the body, allows an impotent man to have erections for intercourse. There are three types of penile prostheses available: malleable rod, self-contained hydraulic, and inflatable, an elaborate device designed to mimic as closely as possible the process of an erection.

Q: How does an inflatable prosthesis work?

A: In addition to the penile implant, it involves a fluid-filled reservoir, implanted under the abdominal muscles, and a pump, placed in the scrotum. When the man wants an erection, he squeezes the pump, moving fluid from the reservoir to the cylinders. When he presses another site on the pump, the fluid leaves the cylinders and returns to the reservoir, and the penis relaxes.

Q: What are the pros and cons of each treatment?

A: You're probably shuddering at the notion of sticking a needle into your penis, but it's not as bad as you think; you inject into the side, where there's spongy tissue with no nerve endings. Still, there are risks. Injections may lead to uncomfortable scarring. If you inject too much of the drug, the erection may last too long and kill penile tissue. Although most urologists prescribe it, injection therapy hasn't yet been approved by the Food and Drug Administration.

The vacuum device is simple and safe. It's often preferred by older men who don't insist on completely rigid erections.

For a number of reasons, the prostheses have fallen out of favor recently. They require surgery, which is expensive and can lead to complications, and there's always a slight risk that the device may malfunction. Some doctors prescribe them as a last resort for men who can't or won't use the other methods.

You can obtain more information about treatment for impotence from one of the groups listed at the end of this book.

Q: Does nerve-sparing prostatectomy eliminate all the cancer?

A: There's some concern that, in the effort to preserve the nerves that control erections, surgeons have been leaving "margins" of cancer. While that hasn't been proven, research has found that nerve-sparing prostatectomies left positive margins in 75 percent of men with stage C cancer. So some experts believe that nerve-sparing surgery should be reserved for younger men with tumors in the earlier stages.

Q: You said there's temporary incontinence after a radical prostatectomy. How often does it become permanent?

A: The nerve-sparing approach to radical prostatectomies now includes several modifications that lower the risk of incontinence. In the same study we cited earlier, Walsh reported that 92 percent of the patients had recovered complete urinary control, and 6 percent had mild stress incontinence—a condition we describe in Chapter 3. The problem was more severe in another 2 percent, but no one was totally incontinent.

Q: Are there other complications or side effects?

A: This isn't one likely to bother most men with prostate cancer but, for the record, we'll note that

men are permanently sterile after radical prostatectomies. This is because removal of the entire prostate gland, including the prostatic urethra, eliminates any place that the sperm can be deposited. So as part of the operation, the vas deferens are tied off.

Q: Do I need radiation or hormonal therapy after a radical prostatectomy?

A: If the surgery was for a cure, and the surgeon tells you he got the tumor out, you may not receive further treatment. It's not uncommon, however, for men with early-stage cancer to undergo radiation after a radical prostatectomy. Many studies have shown that the combination reduces the rate of local recurrence, and there are indications that it improves the rate of survival.

Hormonal therapy would be prescribed as adjuvant treatment—that is, it would be used if, despite the prostatectomy and/or radiation, the tumor spreads outside the prostatic capsule.

Q: Are there other surgical approaches?

A: There's some interest in cryosurgery, the low-temperature technology we talk about in Chapter 3. In this procedure, probes filled with liquid nitrogen are inserted into the prostate. They freeze and destroy the entire prostate, as well as the surrounding tissue and structures such as the seminal vesicles if they're also cancerous. The dead tissue is left in place and eventually reabsorbed by the body.

Q: Who should have cryosurgery?

A: The approach is being tried on men who can't undergo more conventional treatment because they're too ill or they've already had surgery or radiation. One of cryosurgery's major advantages, compared with those two options, is that it can be performed more than once on patients who still have residual cancer after initial treatment.

If the therapy continues to produce good results, says Gary Onik, M.D., an interventional radiologist at Allegheny General Hospital, in Pittsburgh, where cryosurgery has been used effectively, "it will be the first-line treatment of choice." At this point, however, it's still experimental.

RADIATION THERAPY

Q: How is radiation applied to prostate cancer?

A: Radiation therapy, or radiotherapy, uses high-energy rays to shrink tumors and stop cancer cells from growing. Like surgery, it's local therapy—it affects only the cells in the treated area.

Q: How is it delivered?

A: There are two kinds of radiation therapy. Both would be administered by a radiologist or radiation oncologist, who would plan and supervise the treatment.

The more common is **external-beam radiotherapy**, in which a machine aims rays at the tumor and the pelvic area. Typically you'd receive this radiation by going to a hospital five days a week for six or seven weeks.

Q: What's the second kind of radiation therapy?

A: It's radiotherapy that's delivered internally, by radioactive material that's implanted as "seeds" or "pellets" in and around the prostate. Internal radiation therapy is also known as **brachytherapy** or **interstitial radiation therapy**.

There is a growing variety of implants. Some are left in place permanently, while others are removed after they've served their purpose. The kind of tumor determines the choice of implant. Some names you may hear are palladium-103 and iodine-125, two widely used permanent implants that emit low-energy radiation over a period of a couple of weeks or a couple of months, respectively; gold-198, which releases energy at an extremely high rate for a few days; and iridium-192, a high-energy, temporary implant.

Q: How are the seeds implanted?

A: They can be injected through needles with the help of ultrasound, or by means of an open procedure—either suprapubic or retropubic. If the doctor uses needles, it's a quick procedure under a spinal anesthetic. As many as 80 seeds may be implanted in an hour.

Q: Isn't it dangerous to walk around with radioactive isotopes?

A: Initially, you wouldn't be walking around a lot. With iridium-192, you'd probably be quarantined in a hospital room for at least two months, with special precautions to protect nursing staff. With lower-energy implants, you'd be sent home but told to remain somewhat isolated from other people, to avoid exposing them to excess doses of radiation. For the first 17 days of palladium, for example, you must keep your distance from pregnant women and not let a young child sit in your lap for more than five minutes at a time.

How long you're sequestered depends on the half-life of the implant (the length of time that it's highly radioactive). Once the radioactivity wears off, however, you don't need to worry about exposing others. Men with permanent implants can have sexual intercourse with no risk to their partners.

Q: Which radiation therapy is more effective?

A: Choosing between the two different forms of radiation—external beam and internal—and then making a further choice among the various implants is a highly complicated decision that ultimately must be left to the experts. It depends primarily on the kind of tumor that's being treated. Increasingly, implants are being used to treat large, bulky tumors, to ensure that the radiation is delivered primarily to the tumor rather than to normal tissue.

Q: Are the two kinds of radiotherapy ever combined?

A: Often, if the implants are temporary. One of the implants we've mentioned, iridium-192, has been combined with external-beam radiation in several studies. In one of the largest studies, at California's Long Beach Memorial Medical Center, researchers report an excellent survival rate for men who had the combined therapies. However, other experts caution that more studies are needed to confirm that the combination was really superior to conventional external-beam radiation alone.

Q: What are the side effects of radiation?

A: External radiation therapy may produce diarrhea, cramping and intestinal ulcers, all of which typically clear up within weeks after treatment ends. It has also led, in various studies, to permanent impotence in 20 to 50 percent of the men who undergo treatment.

Implants don't usually lead to impotence, but there are sometimes severe complications, such as perforated rectums, when the seeds are implanted. And they have been blamed for temporary urinary difficulties similar to those of BPH.

Q: What about nausea or burns? Aren't those typical side effects?

A: Radiation therapy usually causes fatigue, and the kinds of therapy used in prostate cancer are no exception. However, many of the adverse side effects generally associated with radiation therapy for other cancers don't pertain to radiotherapy for prostate cancer.

With external-beam radiation, the skin over the target area may turn red or become dry. But because the radiation is aimed precisely, patients don't get the burns, hair loss or nausea that often result when other parts of the body are irradiated. And there's no indication that it causes other tumors to develop.

Q: Aside from tumor type, are there other reasons to choose one radiation therapy over the other?

A: Not everybody can use implants. It's out of the question for a man whose rectum has been removed, because the prostate probe has to be placed through the rectum. Men can't have implants if they have large prostates (and would need too many seeds), or have had prior prostate surgery and don't have enough tissue to hold the seeds.

Q: Who should have radiation therapy?

A: The traditional view is that it should be limited to men whose cancer is confined to the prostate and surrounding tissues. That's stages A2, B, and C.

Some doctors, however, believe that radiation is also effective when the cancer has spread to local lymph nodes. That's stage D1. A study by researchers at the Medical College of Wisconsin reported that, when D1 patients received radiation, 61 percent were disease-free at 5 years, and 48 percent at 10 years. Those are better-than-average survival statistics.

Q: Which is better, surgery or radiation?

A: That depends on several factors, including who's doing the procedure. Patients who receive radiation tend to have much the same outcome regardless of where they're treated, while—as we said earlier—a person undergoing nerve-sparing prostatectomy fares better in the hands of an expert surgeon.

Studies show that, for men with stages A2 and B1 cancer, either external radiation or a radical prostatectomies seem to produce the same outcome over a 15-year period. That's the case even though residual cancer has been reported in 30 to 50 percent of men who had radical prostatectomies, and in 60 to 90 percent of men who had radiation therapy.

Q: Residual cancer sounds bad. What is it?

A: It's microscopic tumors found by biopsy, several months after the treatment. This doesn't mean that the tumor has recurred, rather that it's extremely difficult to eradicate completely.

Q: Is it fatal?

A: While failure to "cure" can be fatal in other cancers, it's not at all clear how dangerous it is in the case of prostate cancer. As we said in Chapter 2, it's very common to find microscopic prostate tumors in autopsies of men who have died of other causes.

However, if the PSA level—that measure of tumor growth that we discuss in Chapter 2—is elevated or rising, there's a good chance both you and your doctor will want to make another attack on the cancer with an adjuvant therapy, such as hormonal therapy.

HORMONAL THERAPY

Q: What's hormonal therapy?

A: As we discuss in Chapter 2, prostate cancer depends on androgens, or male hormones, to grow. Hormonal therapy deprives the cancer cells of androgens. Unlike radical prostatectomy or radiation, it's **systemic** therapy, meaning that it can reach cancer cells throughout the body.

There are two forms of hormonal therapy, and sometimes they're administered together. One involves taking hormones that stop the testicles from producing testosterone, the principal androgen. The other involves surgery.

Q: What's the surgical approach?

A: It's a **bilateral orchiectomy**, a procedure in which both testes are removed, generally through a single incision in the scrotal bag. That eliminates the main source of male hormones. It's a very simple procedure that can be done under local anesthesia and, because the scrotum is surprisingly insensitive to pain, it causes little postoperative discomfort. So that the scrotum appears intact, some men choose to have prostheses: soft plastic balls that resemble the testicles in size and consistency.

Q: What's the other hormonal therapy? I suppose I take estrogen?

A: Estrogen therapy isn't used much anymore, partly because it's been established that it increases a man's risk of heart problems, including the formation of blood clots. The therapy that's overtaken estrogen and, increasingly, orchiectomy, is **luteinizing hormone-releasing hormone (LHRH) analog**.

Q: What is LHRH?

A: LHRH is a hormone that normally controls the production of sex hormones. LHRH analogs, which are made in the laboratory, are like LHRH, but instead prevent the testicles from producing testosterone.

LHRH analogs are given by daily or monthly injection. One widely used LHRH analog is leuprolide (sold as Lupron by TAP Pharmaceuticals, or as Zoladex by ICI).

Q: How fast do the LHRH analogs work?

A: Strangely enough, when they're first taken, they lead to higher testosterone levels and tumor growth, or what's known as "flare." This actually worsens some symptoms, including pain. But after about a week, testosterone levels fall to near zero, about the level achieved when both testes are removed. Tumor growth slows down, and the patient's condition improves.

Q: Does the LHRH analog eliminate all testosterone and other androgens?

A: The adrenal glands still produce small amounts of male hormones. Sometimes the patient is given pills that contain an **antiandrogen**, a drug that blocks the effect of any remaining male hormones. One of these antiandrogens is flutamide (brand name Eulexin, manufactured by Schering-Plough). Finasteride, which we describe in Chapter 3 as a treatment for BPH, is another.

Q: Do I really need two kinds of hormone drugs?

A: It's unclear and somewhat controversial. The Food and Drug Administration approved the combined therapy in 1989, after studies showed that men treated with both typically lived for 35 months after treatment, rather than the average 28 months. However, other studies have found little or no benefit in using antiandrogens, except to suppress the initial tumor flare during the first week or so after patients start the LHRH analog.

Q: What are the side effects of hormonal therapy?

A: Many men (perhaps you're among them!) expect the worst: a high soprano voice, enlarged breasts, loss of facial hair. Happily, that's no longer true. Men may get hot flashes with both LHRH analog and orchiectomy. These can be extremely bothersome, but to an extent they can be treated with medication. Sometimes incontinence is a complication.

Men who receive estrogen or an antiandrogen may have nausea, vomiting or tender and swollen breasts. However, these can also be treated.

Q: But doesn't hormonal therapy result in impotence?

A: Yes, far more often than nerve-sparing prostatec- tomies do. Both types of hormonal therapies are considered castration: One is surgical, the other is medical. Most men are impotent after the procedure, and even those who aren't may lose sexual desire.

Q: What about the psychological effect?

A: Most men dread and fear the prospect of an orchi- ectomy, according to many veteran urologists, and its effect can sometimes be traumatic. To many men, even elderly men who haven't had sexual relations for years, an orchiectomy is nothing less than emasculation. So is therapy with hormones, of course; but in theory, at least, that's reversible. An orchiectomy is not.

Q: Any other drawbacks?

A: Taking hormones is extremely expensive. A monthly shot of an LHRH analog costs more than $300. Throw in an antiandrogen, and you're looking at upwards of $500 a month. A bilateral orchiectomy, on the other hand, costs between $2,000 and $3,000, including surgeon's fees and associated hospital costs. That's a range for the country; obviously, you may pay more in some regions than in others.

Q: What do I do if my health insurance doesn't cover that, or if I don't have health insurance?

A: If you meet specific qualifications for low income, you may be eligible to receive Eulexin through an "indigent needs" program offered by Schering. You must apply through your personal physician, who should then contact a local Schering sales representative for the necessary application forms and instructions.

Other pharmaceuticals manufacturers have similar programs. For more information, ask your physician.

Q: Who should have hormonal therapy?

A: The traditional answer is men whose cancer has spread outside the prostatic capsule, to the lymph nodes, other tissues or organs, or to bone. Doctors may also recommend it to men with stage C cancer who can't have surgery or radiation. They might receive hormonal therapy, for example, if they're having trouble urinating because their tumors are compressing their urethras.

Some researchers theorize that, since prostate cancer evidently requires the presence of androgens for growth, hormonal therapy should be used when the cancer is still in its early stages. However, there aren't any studies that support early use.

Q: Which type of hormonal therapy is better (or worse)—the orchiectomy or the injections?

A: Clinical studies have shown that they're equally effective in controlling prostate cancer, so the decision comes down partly to economics, partly to personal preference. One study produced the unsurprising finding that, faced with a choice between orchiectomy and injections, a large majority of men chose injections.

DRUG THERAPY

Q: Speaking of medications, aren't there any drugs that act directly on the tumor?

A: Until very recently, the answer would have been a flat "no." But now researchers are getting some interesting results with an experimental drug called suramin, which was first used decades ago against a tropical parasite.

In clinical trials, the National Cancer Institute has given suramin to 38 men whose prostate cancers had resisted hormonal treatment and had begun to spread to other tissues. NCI found that men treated with the drug had an 85 percent probability of living at least one year, compared with a 20 percent probability for men who didn't receive suramin.

Another study, by researchers at the University of Maryland, reports that suramin appeared to shrink the prostate gland—and thus, presumably, the tumor—in about three-quarters of the 33 men with metastatic prostate cancer.

Q: Are there any drawbacks to suramin?

A: Suramin can have some powerful side effects. Among other things, it can damage the adrenal glands, which are on top of the kidneys and help regulate blood pressure by controlling water retention. In the Maryland drug trials, although researchers used a new computer-aided method of tailoring dosages to individual patients, the side effects were so severe that treatment had to be limited in 28 of the 37 patients. (The other four patients had different types of advanced cancers.)

Q: Is chemotherapy used much against prostate cancer?

A: Chemotherapy, which involves the use of different chemicals or drugs to kill cancer cells, hasn't proved too successful against prostate cancer. Sometimes it's administered to patients who have responded poorly to hormone therapy, as a means of controlling pain. To date, there's no evidence that it prolongs survival.

Q: What are the drawbacks?

A: That depends in part on which drugs are used. In general, however, people who receive chemotherapy may find that they're more susceptible to infection. Other side effects can include loss of appetite, nausea, vomiting or mouth sores. They may also have less energy and may lose their hair.

OTHER THERAPIES

Q: Are there any new therapies you haven't mentioned?

A: Biological therapies, which include biological response modifiers (BRM) and immunotherapy, are different from chemotherapy because they try to increase your own body's ability to fight the cancer.

Probably the best-known BRM therapy involves interferons, chemicals the body makes as a normal response to viral or other infections. A person with cancer may be given much larger amounts of interferon, made in biotechnology laboratories, to boost, direct, or restore his body's natural defenses against the tumor.

Immunotherapy uses antibodies that recognize and attach themselves to the tumor and kill cancer cells. To increase the effectiveness of this approach, antibodies may be linked to radioactive compounds or to chemo-therapy drugs.

However, biological therapies are still in the experi-mental stage and their roles in treating prostate cancer are unknown.

Q: **Are there side effects to biological therapies?**

A: Biological therapies tend to cause flulike symp-toms, such as chills, fever, muscleaches, weakness, loss of appetite, nausea, vomiting or diarrhea.

Q: **Are there any therapies I can try myself to fight prostate cancer?**

A: Many of the alternative techniques that have been used against other cancers, such as biofeedback and visualization—in which you use your mind to try to control the spread of, or even to shrink, the tumor—obviously can be tried with prostate cancer. These can be learned from some psychotherapists.

As with any cancer, men with prostate cancer have sought and tried miracle "cures," including vitamins and fad foods; one urged on Cornelius Ryan, as he recounted in *A Private Battle,* was Eskimo soup made from the blood and guts of various animals.

Q: Isn't a macrobiotic diet supposed to help fight prostate cancer, or cancer in general?

A: You may be thinking of the case of Anthony J. Sattilaro, a Philadelphia physician and president of Methodist Hospital who was diagnosed with metastatic prostate cancer in 1978, at the age of 47. Sattilaro, who received a bilateral orchiectomy and hormonal treatment, tried a macrobiotic diet and felt it helped him so much that he promoted it widely.

A macrobiotic diet consists primarily of whole grains like brown rice, along with some vegetables, beans and seaweed. It excludes all meat, dairy products, sugar, oils and synthetic chemicals and preservatives.

By 1982, when Sattilaro completed his book, *Recalled by Life,* and gave the diet wide publicity, his cancer was in total remission. Ultimately, he died of prostate cancer, but it wasn't until 1989, a remarkable 11 years after his initial diagnosis.

Q: Does that prove a macrobiotic diet helped Sattilaro?

A: Cancer specialists believe that his improvement was due to the surgery and additional hormone treatment. In fact, some doctors say a macrobiotic diet can actually be harmful because it's low in vitamins and minerals that people need and doesn't allow vitamin and mineral supplements.

NONTREATMENT

Q: Nontreatment: That's self-evident, right? No treatment?

A: Basically that's right, although the term "non-treatment" is something of a misnomer. Patients who choose not to be treated may still receive hormonal therapy if their tumors progress and they develop symptoms. That's why watchful waiting may be a more precise description of what actually takes place.

Q: Are there any studies supporting watchful waiting?

A: Yes, in 1992 researchers in Sweden published a landmark study of 223 men with early, untreated prostate cancer. The average age at diagnosis was 72. A 10-year follow-up showed survival rates similar to those of men who received standard intervention—either radical prostatectomy or radiation. Of the 124 men who died during the decade, only 19 died from prostate cancer. Based on their findings, the researchers concluded that radical prostatectomies of early-stage prostatic cancer should be considered experimental.

Q: So nontreatment is preferable?

A: That's certainly one conclusion, although the results should be viewed as cautiously as any other research findings. For example, Joseph Oesterling, of the Mayo Clinic, has remarked that most of the men in the Swedish study were older and had a shorter life expectancy than would be the case for men with diagnosed cancer as part of a large-scale screening program in the United States.

Q: Is there any study involving younger men?

A: Unfortunately, there aren't any comparable studies on men under the age of 60. But one recent study, which otherwise gave strong support for a "wait-and-see" approach, did offer some support for intervention in certain cases. Published in the *Journal of the American Medical Association* in 1993, the research looked at men ages 60 to 75 years with stages A and B prostate cancer. The researchers reported that the men ages 60 to 65 years did benefit from treatment like prostatectomy or radiation, if their tumors were relatively aggressive.

For the study, the Prostate Patient Outcomes Research Team, which includes researchers from a number of medical establishments, measured the benefit of treatment in terms of "quality-adjusted life expectancy"—"quality" being an aggregate measure of impotence, incontinence and other complications of both cancer and its treatment. The study found that relatively younger men with faster-growing localized tumors could gain up to 3.5 years in quality-adjusted life expectancy if they chose a radical prostatectomy or radiation therapy over watchful waiting.

The marginal benefit of treatment, however, dipped sharply—to less than a year—when the tumor was slow growing. For older men, the gain in quality-adjusted life expectancy was less than six months. And for some patients, nontreatment was clearly preferable to treatment.

Q: What if the cancer is in stage C or D? Is treatment better than watchful waiting?

A: There's no clear evidence about the impact of treatment on stage C tumors. But a recent study by researchers at the Memorial Sloan-Kettering Cancer Center did look into nontreatment in the case of 35 men with newly diagnosed stage D prostate cancer but with minimal symptoms of disease. It compared the quality of life of patients who received hormonal therapy when they were diagnosed, with that of men who decided to defer treatment until their PSA levels or symptoms worsened. (In this case, "quality of life" included elements like the patients' social life, feelings of well-being and anxiety, and independence.)

Researchers found that the group that opted for deferred treatment had fewer sexual problems and more physical energy than the group that had hormonal therapy. After six months, the group being treated was suffering more psychological distress. Concerning the group that chose not to be treated, the researchers wrote, "quality of survival was equally important to overall survival time."

Survival itself wasn't an issue in the study. The data were drawn from questionnaires completed by the patients themselves, over a period of six months after they made their initial decision about treatment.

Q: Are there any side effects of nontreatment, as long as the tumor remains localized?

A: In one study, approximately one-third of patients required at least one transurethral prostatectomy, or TURP, the procedure we describe in Chapter 3, for the relief of bladder outlet obstructions. However, it's not entirely certain that cancer growth was responsible for the obstructions.

Q: Is TURP safe for cancer patients?

A: The answer would have to be "yes, but . . . ." Studies have connected TURP to an increase in metastasis and a decrease in survival for patients whose cancer hadn't yet metastasized at the time they had the procedure. Researchers found they could reduce the risk somewhat by lowering the pressure they used in irrigating.

(During a TURP, the surgical area is regularly flushed with fluid, to keep it clear of blood.)

In a recent article in *Ca,* the American Cancer Society's publication for clinicians, two physicians who looked at this problem conclude that, if TURP is absolutely necessary to relieve a patient's obstruction, his doctor should consider radiating the tumor once to reduce its size and the likelihood that it would spread during the procedure.

Q: Are there other complications from TURP?

A: In addition to the various side effects we describe in Chapter 3, there are potentially more severe complications when prostate cancer is involved. As the prostate becomes filled with tumor, the prostatic urethra turns into a rigid tube. As a result, about 5 percent of patients who have TURP to relieve obstructions from advanced prostatic cancer develop incontinence problems.

Severe bleeding during a TURP can also be a greater problem than with BPH patients, because certain substances in the cancerous tissue promote bleeding and prevent blood clotting.

Q: Are there any alternatives to TURP for someone with prostate cancer?

A: One recent study found that transrectal microwave hyperthermia, the heat therapy we describe in Chapter 3, is actually more effective in relieving bladder obstruction in men with prostate cancer than in men who have only BPH. The researchers report that five weeks of heat therapy led to relief over the following two years, and 80 percent of the subjects reported an improvement in quality of life.

TREATMENT ACCORDING TO STAGE

Q: How do I figure out which treatment is best for me?

A: That's a decision you must make in consultation with your doctor and family. If you consult with more than one doctor, you may hear more than one opinion. As we said earlier, there's considerable disagreement within medical circles about which treatments are most effective.

But what we can tell you in this section are the most common treatments for each stage, as indicated by the National Cancer Institute. Note the wide range of options. In each case, however, you should keep in mind that nontreatment, or watchful waiting, is always an option, regardless of your age or health.

Q: What's the treatment for stage A prostate cancer?

A: That depends on whether you have stage A1 or stage A2 cancer. If you have the less malignant A1 cancer, in which microscopic cancer cells are found in only one area of your prostate, and if you're older, your doctor may follow you closely without any treatment. She may choose this option for you because your cancer is not causing any symptoms or other problems and may be growing slowly. If you are younger, you may have a radical prostatectomy or external radiation therapy.

Q: What if it's stage A2 cancer?

A: If it's stage A2 cancer, where cancer cells may be detected microscopically in many areas of the prostate, your treatment may be one of the following:

1) External radiation therapy

2) Radical prostatectomy, usually with pelvic lymph node dissection. Radiation therapy may be given after surgery in some cases.

3) A clinical trial of internal radiation therapy, often in addition to pelvic lymph node dissection

4) Nontreatment, if you are older or have another, more serious illness. In this case, your doctor may follow you closely without treatment.

5) A clinical trial of external radiation therapy using new techniques to protect your normal tissues from radiation.

Q: What about stage B?

A: If you have stage B cancer, which is still contained within the prostate and is typically detected during a routine rectal exam, your treatment may be one of the following:

1) Radical prostatectomy, usually with pelvic lymph node dissection. Radiation therapy may be given following surgery.

2) External radiation therapy

3) A clinical trial of internal radiation therapy, often in addition to pelvic lymph node dissection

4) Nontreatment, if you are older or have another more serious illness. Your doctor may choose this option for you because your cancer is not causing any symptoms or other problems and may be growing slowly.

5) A clinical trial of external radiation therapy using new techniques to protect your normal tissues from radiation. Other clinical trials are testing new types of radiation.

Q: What's the treatment for stage C?

A: In the case of stage C cancer, which is still localized but may extend beyond the prostatic capsule to involve the seminal vesicles as well, your treatment may be one of the following:

1) External radiation therapy, including clinical trials for new types of radiation

2) Radical prostatectomy and usually pelvic lymph node dissection. Radiation therapy may be given following surgery.

3) Nontreatment, if you are older or have another more serious illness. Your doctor may choose this option for you because your cancer is not causing any symptoms or other problems and may be growing slowly.

4) A clinical trial of internal radiation therapy, often in addition to pelvic lymph node dissection.

If you're unable to undergo surgery or radiation therapy, your doctor may give you treatments to relieve symptoms, such as problems urinating. In this case, your treatment may be one of the following:

1) Radiation therapy to relieve symptoms

2) TURP

3) Hormone therapy.

Q: Stage D?

A: Your treatment depends on whether you have stage D1 or stage D2 prostate cancer. If you have stage D1 cancer, in which the tumor has spread immediately outside the prostate or to the pelvic lymph nodes, your treatment may be one of the following:

1) External radiation therapy, including clinical trials for new forms of radiation. Hormone therapy may be given in addition to radiation.

2) Radical prostatectomy and orchiectomy

3) Nontreatment, if you are older or have another more serious illness. Your doctor may choose this option for you because your cancer is not causing any symptoms or other problems and may be growing slowly.

4) A clinical trial of hormone therapy.

Q: Then what about stage D2?

A: If you have stage D2 disease, in which the cancer has spread far from the prostate to, say, the lungs, the bones or the liver, your treatment may be one of the following:

1) Hormone therapy

2) External-beam radiation therapy to relieve symptoms

3) TURP to relieve symptoms

4) A clinical trial of chemotherapy or new forms of hormone therapy

5) Your doctor may follow you closely and wait until you develop symptoms before giving you treatment.

Q: What if the tumor recurs?

A: Your treatment depends on many things, including what treatment you had before. If you had a radical prostatectomy and the cancer comes back in only a small area, you may receive radiation therapy. If the disease has spread to other parts of your body, you will probably undergo hormone therapy. Radiation therapy may be given, as well, to relieve symptoms such as bone pain. You may also choose to take part in a clinical trial of chemotherapy or biological therapy.

FOLLOW-UP AND RECURRENCE

Q: How is the cancer monitored?

A: Whatever treatment—or nontreatment—you choose, you'll have regular follow-up exams. If the cancer was confined to the prostate, your doctor will want to make sure that it hasn't returned. If it has spread beyond the prostate, you should be examined to see what other medical care is necessary.

The doctor will want to know whether you've had any changes in appetite, any urinary problems, dramatic weight fluctuations or bone pain, all of which could indicate metastasis. We've discussed many of the tests and procedures elsewhere in this book, because they're also diagnostic tools.

Q: What tests are performed?

A: The doctor should perform a rectal exam to check for new nodules. He'll run a PSA test. PSA levels should be undetectable unless disease remains. In fact, the PSA test was first used to confirm the success of a radical prostatectomy. There'll be a urinalysis and possibly other blood tests to determine if your liver and kidneys are functioning properly.

You may have an annual bone scan and bone x-ray to see whether the cancer has spread. If you have prostatic bleeding, which shows up in your urine, your doctor might use a cystoscope to locate its source and also to assess the degree of obstruction to urine flow caused by the tumor.

Q: What happens if the cancer has metastasized?

A: You will be treated for any symptoms and side effects caused by the metastatic tumor itself. These symptoms will be different for each patient, depending on the location of the metastasis. However, some of the more common problems are due to metastasis to bones, especially the spine or skull, or to the brain.

If the growing tumor presses on the spinal cord, it can cause a condition called spinal cord compression; symptoms include back pain, muscle weakness, decreased sensation, and loss of bowel or bladder function. This is a medical emergency that must be treated immediately to reduce the risk of permanent neurological injury. Usually you'd get medication, followed by either radiation or surgery.

If the tumor metastasizes to the skull or brain, headache, seizures or other neurological problems may develop. Like the problems caused by spinal cord compression, these are also emergency conditions that require immediate medical attention.

Q: How is pain handled?

A: Pain management can be an important part of care for men with prostate cancer. Depending on the metastasis, your doctor may use radiation, hormonal therapy or other approaches to shrink the tumor.

The trouble is that the treatments themselves can produce other problems. Radiation therapy directed to the base of the skull, for example, can produce irreversible neurologic injury, and the pain relief is temporary.

Recently, there has been some interest in **radiopharmaceuticals**, such as strontium-89, a radioactive element that is given by vein and builds up in high concentrations in metastases within bone. These drugs may be less toxic than external radiation, and relieve pain significantly.

However, they're no substitute for conventional radiation therapy in preventing spinal cord compression.

Doctors also use anti-inflammatory drugs in combination with morphine to treat pain. Keep in mind that not all drugs are equally effective against all cancers; what works for metastatic bone pain from breast cancer, for example, may not be effective against metastatic bone pain from prostate cancer.

Metastases to the hip and pelvis often produce local pain that's exacerbated by movement, especially during weight-bearing movement. In addition to radiation therapy, your doctor may try to control the pain through orthopedic measures, such as pinning and otherwise stabilizing the bone.

Q: What if my cancer resists therapy?

A: In that case, you may want to consider, and discuss with your family and physician, issues regarding quality of life versus measures to prolong life.

If you decide you don't want to treat the tumor further, your doctor can suggest ways that you can receive symptomatic relief and support outside of the hospital. In the past decade, there's been a tremendous development of facilities and techniques that allow you to remain in your home. A vast home-health infrastructure can provide comprehensive nursing care and supervision, as well as psychological support.

Alternatively, you may wish to participate in cancer treatment trials of drugs or other approaches that are highly experimental and of unknown benefit. You can ask NCI or your doctor to put you in touch with large cancer centers that are running such trials.

INFORMATIONAL AND MUTUAL-AID GROUPS

Agency for Health Care Policy and Research
Publications Clearinghouse
P.O. Box 8547
Silver Springs, MD 20907
800-358-9295

American Cancer Society
1599 Clifton Rd., N.E.
Atlanta, GA 30329
800-ACS-2345
   (Check your telephone directory for an ACS office
   in your city or state.)

Help for Incontinent People (HIP)
P.O. Box 544
Union, SC 29379
800-BLADDER

Impotence Institute of America, Inc.
2020 Pennsylvania Ave. N.W., Suite 292
Washington, DC 20006
800-669-1603

National Cancer Institute
National Institutes of Health
Bethesda, MD 20892
800-4-CANCER

National Institute on Aging
Information Center
P.O. Box 8057
Gaithersburg, MD 20898
800-222-2225

**National Kidney and Urologic Diseases
    Information Clearinghouse**
Box NKUDIC
9000 Rockville Pike
Bethesda, MD 20892
301-468-6345

**Patient Advocates for Advanced Cancer
    Treatments (PAACT)**
1143 Parmelee, N.W.
Grand Rapids, MI 49504
616-453-1477

Prostate Health Council
c/o American Foundation for Urologic Disease, Inc.
300 W. Pratt St., Suite 401
Baltimore, MD 21201
800-242-2383

The Simon Foundation
P.O. Box 815
Wilmette, IL 60091
800-23-SIMON
    (for incontinence)

US TOO Prostate Cancer Survivor Support Group
800-82-US-TOO
    Same address as Prostate Health Council (see above)

GLOSSARY

Acute bacterial prostatitis: A rare and serious prostatic disease that results from a sudden infusion of bacteria into the prostate.

Acute urinary retention: A condition, sometimes triggered by alcohol, cold, immobility or certain medications, in which a man suddenly finds himself completely unable to urinate.

Adjuvant: Treatment that is offered after the most effective form of therapy has been tried.

Alpha-adrenergic blockers: A group of drugs that relax the smooth muscle tissue in both the prostate and the bladder neck, thus easing constriction of the urethra.

Analgesics: Pain-relief medications.

Androgens: A class of male hormones.

Antiandrogen: A drug that, as part of hormonal therapy, blocks the effect of any remaining androgens.

Antihypertensive: Blood pressure-lowering medication that, because it also relaxes muscles, is sometimes prescribed for benign prostatic hyperplasia.

Anus: The opening of the rectum where solid waste leaves the body.

Aromatase: An enzyme that converts testosterone into the form of estrogen that is found in men and is thought to contribute to BPH.

Artificial insemination: A reproductive technique in which sperm is extracted from a man after ejaculation and then deposited in a woman's vagina.

Artificial urinary sphincter: A device designed to restore control to an incontinent person by giving him the mechanical means of opening and closing his urethra.

Aspiration: The removal of fluids by suction, often through a needle that is attached to a syringe.

Bacterial prostatitis: Prostatitis, or inflammation of the prostate, caused by bacteria.

Balloon dilatation: See **Balloon urethroplasty**.

Balloon urethroplasty (or Balloon dilatation): A balloon treatment of the urethra to compress the prostate and widen the urethra, easing the flow of urine.

Benign prostatic hyperplasia (BPH): A noncancerous enlargement of the prostate through the multiplication of the number of cells. Occurring mainly in elderly men, the overgrowth of prostate tissue may push against the urethra and the bladder, blocking the flow of urine and causing acute discomfort.

Beta-carotene: A compound, found in foods, that can be converted in the body to an active form of vitamin A.

Bilateral orchiectomy: A procedure in which both testes are removed, generally through an incision in the scrotal bag, to eliminate the main source of male hormones and slow the spread of prostate cancer.

Biofeedback: A technique in which a person learns to consciously control involuntary responses, such as muscle contractions, by having these responses initially monitored electronically.

Biopsy: Removal of a small tissue sample for microscopic examination.

Bladder: The hollow organ in the lower abdomen where urine is stored.

Bladder catheterization: A diagnostic or therapeutic procedure in which a thin rubber tube is inserted up the urethra into the bladder.

Blood-prostate barrier: The portion of the prostate that prevents certain substances from entering, and effectively keeps out most antibiotics, making it difficult to treat infections.

Bone scan: A highly sensitive process that uses a radioactive substance to image the bone structure.

Brachytherapy (or Interstitial radiation therapy): Internal radiation therapy, generated by radioactive material implanted as ''seeds'' or ''pellets'' in and around the cancerous area, such as in the prostate.

Catheterize: To insert a tubular medical device (catheter) into a canal, vessel, passageway or body cavity, usually to inject or withdraw fluids or to keep a passage open.

Cellule: A small pouch that develops between trabeculations.

Chlamydia: The most common sexually transmitted disease, a bacterial infection acquired chiefly through vaginal or anal intercourse.

Chronic bacterial prostatitis: A recurring bacterial infection in the prostate.

Coitus interruptus: The interruption of sexual intercourse, generally for contraceptive purposes, to enable the man to ejaculate outside the vagina.

Colon bacilli: Bacteria that are in the colon.

Compensated bladder: A bladder that empties completely on voiding.

Computerized tomography (CT or CAT) scan: A series of detailed pictures of areas inside the body, created by a computer linked to an x-ray machine.

Congestive prostatitis: See **Prostatostasis**.

Creatinine: A metabolic waste product, the blood level of which is an important measure of kidney function.

Cryosurgery: A surgical procedure employing liquid nitrogen at exceptionally low temperatures to freeze and destroy tissue.

Curative: Potentially capable of completely destroying a cancer.

Cystoscopy: A procedure in which a cystoscope— a slender, hollow tube with a lens at each end— is passed into the penile urethra and bladder, allowing visual examination of the urinary tract.

Decompensated bladder: A bladder that does not empty completely on voiding, so that residual urine remains.

Digital (manual) rectal exam: A procedure in which a doctor inserts a gloved, lubricated finger into the rectum and, through the wall of the rectum, checks the prostate for hard or lumpy areas.

Dihydrotestosterone (DHT): A more active form of testosterone that tends to be highly concentrated in the prostate and has been implicated in the benign enlargement of the prostate.

Diverticula: Pouches or sacs that branch out from the bladder when the bladder muscle is overworked.

Dry orgasm: See **Retrograde ejaculation**.

Epididymis: An elongated, cordlike structure in the testes that stores and transmits sperm.

Epididymitis: Inflammation of the epididymis.

Estrogen: A female hormone.

Excretory urogram (or Intravenous pyelogram [IVP] or **Intravenous urogram [IVU]):** A test performed by the injection of dye that concentrates in the kidneys. A series of x-rays are then taken at timed intervals to provide much information about the entire urinary tract, including the size of the prostate and bladder, and kidney functioning.

External-beam radiotherapy: Radiation therapy delivered from a machine, either a lower-voltage cobalt unit or a higher-voltage linear accelerator.

Fistula: An abnormal connection between two hollow spaces or organs.

5-alpha-reductase: An enzyme that converts testosterone into a more active androgen called dihydrotestosterone.

Foley catheter: A catheter that is placed into the bladder for continuous drainage and left in place by means of a liquid-filled balloon within the bladder.

Gland: An aggregation of cells, specialized to secrete or excrete materials.

Gonorrhea: A sexually transmitted bacterial infection that may involve the urethra.

Growth factors: Proteins that may act on tissue to cause enlargements, such as benign prostatic hyperplasia.

Hematuria: Blood or red blood cells in the urine.

Hesitancy: The condition when a man has to wait for several seconds to a couple of minutes for his urine flow to start while the bladder muscle strains against the resistance of the prostate.

Hormonal therapy: The use of medications or the surgical removal of the testicles to prevent male hormones from stimulating further growth of prostate cancer.

Hyperthermia (or Thermotherapy): The application of microwave heat to the enlarged prostate with the object of shrinking or destroying the BPH tissue.

Impotence: The inability of a male to develop or maintain an erection sufficient to copulate.

Incontinence: A person's inability to control urination.

Intermittency: An involuntary stopping and starting of the urinary stream.

Interstitial radiation therapy: See **Brachytherapy**.

Intravenous pyelogram (IVP): See **Excretory urogram**.

Intravenous urogram: See **Excretory urogram**.

Laparoscopy: The use of small tubes to gain access to the interior of the abdomen. In a laparoscopic pelvic lymph node dissection, a doctor can remove and examine lymph nodes.

Luteinizing hormone-releasing hormone (LHRH) analog: A laboratory-made substance that works against LHRH, which is a hormone that normally controls the production of sex hormones, to eliminate or slow the spread of cancer.

Lymphadenectomy: A biopsy of the lymph nodes.

Lymphangiogram: An imaging procedure in which dye is injected into the lymph system and travels to the pelvic area, concentrating in such a way that an x-ray can reveal cancer in the nodes.

Lymph nodes: Small glands located in many areas of the body that help defend the body against harmful foreign particles. Prostate cancer often spreads first to the pelvic lymph nodes.

Magnetic resonance imaging (MRI): An imaging technique that produces detailed pictures of areas inside the body by linking a computer with a powerful magnet.

Metastasize: Spread, as in the case of cancer, to distant organs or tissues.

Nafarelin acetate: A hormone blocker that inhibits the testes' production of testosterone by acting on the pituitary gland.

Necrosis: The death of living tissue.

Nocturia: The urge or need to urinate at night.

Nonbacterial prostatitis: See **Prostatodynia** and **Prostatostasis**.

Nonspecific urethritis (NSU): An infection of the prostatic urethra.

Palliative: Capable of reducing the symptoms of a disease and slowing its growth, but unable to wipe it out.

Perineum: In a man, the area between the scrotum and the anus.

Prostate: A walnut-size gland in the male reproductive system that surrounds part of the urethra and secretes most of the fluid that is ejaculated with sperm during orgasm.

Prostate cancer: A malignant and hence potentially serious disease of the prostate that accounts for more deaths in men than any other cancer except skin cancer.

Prostatectomy: See **Transurethral resection of the prostate** and **Radical prostatectomy**.

Prostate-specific antigen (PSA): A substance, produced exclusively by prostate cells, whose level increases in the presence of prostatic cancer and rises significantly with metastasis, or spread, of the cancer.

Prostatic acid phosphatase (PAP): Another substance produced by prostate cells; an increase in PAP indicates the spread of prostate cancer.

Prostatic urethra: The portion of the urethra that is within the prostate.

Prostatitis: An inflammation of the prostate, which may or may not be caused by the presence of bacteria.

Prostatodynia: A form of nonbacterial prostatitis, in which pain seems to be coming from the prostate, but is much more likely to be coming from the muscles of the floor of the pelvis, from an inflammation in one or more of the pelvic bones, or from a disease in the rectum.

Prostatostasis (or Congestive prostatitis): The most common form of nonbacterial prostatitis, generally attributed to the accumulation of excess fluid within the prostate.

Prosthesis: A device that, surgically implanted within the body, replicates natural body functions or parts. A penile prosthesis allows an impotent man to have erections for intercourse.

Radiation therapy: The use of high-energy rays to shrink tumors and stop cancer cells from growing. Like surgery, it is local therapy, affecting only the cells in the treated area.

Radical prostatectomy: The complete surgical removal of the prostate, usually for prostatic cancer.

Radiopharmaceuticals: Radioactive drugs used for diagnostic or therapeutic purposes.

Rectum: The portion of the large intestine between the colon and the anus.

Reflux: A potentially dangerous condition in which, due to prostatic growth, urine is unable to leave the bladder through the urethra and eventually backs up into the kidneys.

Renal scan: An image of the kidneys, produced by injecting radioactive material.

Resectoscope: The instrument, used in a TURP, that allows the surgeon to resect, or cut, and remove the obstructing prostatic tissue.

Retrograde ejaculation: Male orgasm without the release of seminal fluid through the penis.

Retropubic: The area behind and below the pubic bone.

Scrotum: The sac of skin that contains the testicles.

Segmented urine culture: A series of tests, typically to check for prostatitis, in which the individual urinates at intervals into three separate cups.

Seminal vesicles: The two saclike structures directly behind the base of the bladder that contribute to the production of semen.

Silent prostatism: An infrequent condition in which a man may be unaware he has a urinary obstruction until he suddenly becomes completely unable to urinate. Untreated, the condition leads to kidney failure, coma and death.

Sonogram: An image obtained by ultrasonic scanning.

Staging: The effort to determine whether a cancer has spread and what parts of the body are involved.

Stent: A stainless-steel device that can be inserted semi-permanently into the prostatic urethra to stretch it and let urine flow more easily.

Stress incontinence: Involuntary release of urine when there is an increase in pressure within the bladder, usually from coughing, laughing or straining.

Stricture: Abnormal narrowing of a bodily passage, often by scarring.

Stroma: The tissue framework, as distinguished from the specific substance, of an organ or gland.

Suprapubic: Above the pubic bone.

Sympathomimetic: A decongestant drug that may, as a side effect, tighten the bladder neck and make it difficult to urinate.

Systemic: Pervading the entire body rather than being limited to an area or organ. Systemic therapy reaches cancer cells throughout the body.

Testicles: The male glands that produce sperm and male hormones.

Testosterone: A male hormone produced mainly by the testicles.

Thermotherapy: See **Hyperthermia**.

Trabeculation: Irregular bands of thickened muscle tissue that develop in the bladder wall as the prostate enlarges and the bladder muscle has to work harder to force out urine.

Transrectal hyperthermia: A procedure in which heat is applied to the prostate by means of a microwave probe inserted through the rectum, to relieve the condition known as BPH.

Transrectal ultrasonography: An examination that produces an image of the prostate by inserting a probe into the rectum to direct sound waves to the prostate.

Transurethral hyperthermia: Same as transrectal hyperthermia, but with the probe inserted through the urethra.

Transurethral incision of the prostate (TUIP): A more limited version of TURP, in which a surgeon makes two incisions from the bladder neck through the prostate to widen the urinary passage, but does not resect the enlarged prostate.

Transurethral resection of the prostate (TURP):
The most common procedure for BPH, in which a surgeon tunnels through the urethra with a resectoscope to cut away the enlarged tissue.

Transurethral ultrasound-guided laser-induced prostatectomy (TULIP): A highly experimental procedure to destroy BPH tissue by inserting a laser probe into the urethra and an ultrasound probe in the rectum to direct the laser energy, which superheats and destroys the tissue.

Ultrasonic aspiration: A highly experimental procedure to improve urine flow in men with BPH by directing ultrasound vibrations against the enlarged portion of the prostate and "disrupting" the tissue. The tissue is then aspirated through the device.

Ultrasound: A procedure that bounces high-frequency sound waves off tissues and converts the echoes into images.

Urea nitrogen: A waste product whose presence in the blood is used to measure kidney function.

Uremic poisoning (or Uremia): A condition arising from kidney failure, which can lead to unconsciousness and death.

Ureters: The two very thin, muscular tubes that transport urine from the kidneys to the bladder.

Urethra: The canal inside the penis through which urine and semen pass as they leave the body.

Urethral sphincter: The muscle located just beyond the prostate, enclosing part of the urethra, that a man voluntarily contracts to shut off his urinary flow.

Urinalysis: The physical, chemical and microscopic analysis of urine for abnormalities.

Urinary retention: A condition in which some urine remains in the bladder, due to a constricted urethra, even after a man has voided.

Urine culture: The incubation of urine at a specific temperature so as to permit the growth and identification of microorganisms.

Urodynamic studies: Quantitative analysis of the two principal functions of the bladder, urine storage and voiding.

Uroflometer: A machine used to conduct a urodynamic evaluation by measuring the rate of urine flow.

Urologist: A physician specializing in diseases of the urinary tract and the male reproductive system.

Vas deferens: The two tubes that carry the sperm from the testes to the urethra.

Vasectomy: An operation, generally for contraceptive purposes, in which the vas deferens are sealed off.

SUGGESTED READING

Chalker, Rebecca, and Kristene E. Whitmore. *Overcoming Bladder Disorders*. New York: Harper & Row, 1990.

Gomella, Leonard G., and John J. Fried. *Recovering From Prostate Cancer*. New York: HarperPaperbacks, 1993.

Greenberger, Monroe E., and Mary-Ellen Siegel. *Dr. Greenberger's What Every Man Should Know About His Prostate*. New York: Walker and Company, 1988.

McAllister, Robert M., Sylvia Teich Horowitz, and Raymond V. Gilden. *Cancer*. New York: BasicBooks, 1993.

Rous, Stephen N. *The Prostate Book: Sound Advice on Symptoms and Treatment*. New York: W.W. Norton, 1992.

Shapiro, Charles E., and Kathleen Doheny. *The Well-Informed Patient's Guide to Prostate Problems*. New York: Dell Publishing, 1993.

Taguchi, Yosh. *Private Parts: A Doctor's Guide to the Male Anatomy*. New York: Doubleday, 1989.

INDEX

B

C